Adams' Laws

42 life lessons gleaned
from a few cultural nodes

Adams' Laws

42 life lessons gleaned from a few cultural nodes

Or, some of the cultural anti-wisdom our society cherishes so deeply and ignores so profoundly.

By

Jeffrey P Adams, XyZ

Adams' Laws: 42 life lessons gleaned from a few cultural nodes.
Copyright 2024, by Jeffrey P. Adams, LLC.
All rights reserved.

 Published by *GETTHEWORDOUT* Press

1st Print Edition ISBN: **978-1-936902-58-3**

Contents

Introduction 1
The Lessons.. 7
The 99.9% Rule.. 8
The *Blue Apple Laws* Law 10
The Dancing Cigarette Box Rule 12
The Death by Convenience Rule or, The Running Water Lesson 17
The For-Profit-Only Rule... 20
The Ford Pinto Lesson 25
The Forest Gump Rule 27
The Fortune Cookie Rule 32
The Good-for-Two-Years Rule 34
The Investor Rule... 37
The IQ 85 Rule... 40
The *It's illegal* Rule 43
The 5G Lesson 45
The Louis, Lewis [Loo'eeeee] Lesson 49
The MCI Lesson... 51
The New & Improved Rule... 53
The OS11 / Win 11 Lesson.. 58
The *Spirit of St Louis* Lesson 60
The Stupid Geniuses Rule 62
The Hill House Rule... 67
The Mrs Grundy Rule 69
The Odysseus Lesson... 71
The "Pacled" Rule.. 73
The Ad Backfire Rule or, Modern Four-Walling 75
The Too Many Lawyers Rule.. 78
The World's Best Clam Chowder Lesson........................... 83
The Wrong Side of the Fence Rule 84
The Brick Layer Rule 86

The "Grasshopper" Rule 87
The Ad Blocker Lesson 89
The Skyrim Rule 91
The *Day After Tomorrow* Lesson 93
The George Harrison Lesson 95
The Xenomorph Lesson 97
The Microsoft Lesson or, Why Corporations Fail 99
The White Album Rule 104
The *Last of the Samurai* Lesson 106
The Plain Hot Dog Lesson 108
The *Banacek* Lesson 110
The MSG Rule 112
The Celebrity Rule 114
The Law of 42 116
Epilogue **118**

Introduction

It's said that "the people have a funny way of deciding for themselves what matters and what doesn't." Actually, no, they don't. Or, rather, *sometimes* they get to decide but more often it is decided for them, by those with significant influence over the public's attention – and attention span.

Things happen. Interesting Things and Amazing Things. Some of these things really are interesting or amazing, all on their own. Some of these things are considered amazing or interesting simply because public attention was directed there with sufficient hoo-haw and harrumphing to convince the Herd that it really was interesting, perhaps even important.

Stuff gets on the news. Some stuff fails to get on the news. Some things get on the news to distract from other things that *should* be on the news. Some things are on the news far too much, so that they become "significant" simply by overexposure.

Example: can a celebrity ever truly have a fair trial? (Quick answer: not in our current system.) OJ Simpson was found innocent, yet almost no one in the public bought it. In fact he was later found guilty in a separate trial, a civil court. That's clearly double-indemnity, yet it was (and is) considered legal[1]. Found innocent, but found irrevocably guilty in the court of public opinion as well as in that civil court. Was it a fair trial? I don't know; I wasn't there. What I do know is that *everyone* had an opinion about it, whether they had been in court hearing all the evidence or not. And they had not. Other celebrities in recent years have been in court with issues – mostly private

---

[1]The justification for that not being double jeopardy is that the two courts are considered two separate jurisdictions. Huh? Call it what you will, he was tried twice on the same charges and lost the 2nd time. More on this later.

issues – subsequently found innocent (or having won the case, one way or another), and yet the news media managed to do significant damage to these people, so that even "winning" they in fact lost. Celebrity trials should automatically be closed to reporters and the general public. (Maybe? Or Maybe not? What do you think?)

Example: the warning "may be hot after heating" now occurs on many packages of microwavable semi-food, coffee cups and other things. *May* be? Does that mean I might "heat it" and yet find it's still cold? (That *is* what it says, you know, absolutely!) No, it means "here there have been lawyers." Or maybe it's a *Keep Off The Grass* sign aimed at predatory lawyers by other lawyers, who might be predators themselves. Or not. Whatever, no one wins a law suit, as law suits have the awful side-effect of raising costs of the product for all consumers from that point on. Perhaps of every product from that company. Sometimes quite a lot. (Why is American medicine so vastly expensive? Besides the fact that it can be, the liability of it all is massive, with all those run-away law suits over the last 50+ years. We *all* pay for those, you know.) A very small number of people, then, end up with some money, perhaps deservedly so, but everyone from then on, including the "winners" now have to share a price hike, perhaps a big one. Costs of law suits and settlements (like corporate taxes and product advertising) are simply passed on to the consumer. In short, while no one actually wins, it's safe to say the corporation at least did not lose[2]. In the long run, society loses on every one of these law suits. I'll admit though that sometimes a law suit is necessary – sometimes it's the only way to get a corporate body to listen and take action, though too often that "action" is little more than placing a "may be hot after heating" message on all packages from then on.

---

[2]In fact, a law suit some times amounts to little more than free publicity.

Example: Legislators seem to think they can repeal the laws of physics. A pedestrian right of way craze went through America several years ago. State after state was passing pedestrian right of way laws, and yet in state after state the pedestrian death rate subsequently went up. Nevertheless states kept passing these laws. How can you expect a ¼ ton (or more) vehicle moving at 30 miles an hour (or more) to be more maneuverable and more able to stop than a 150 pound person moving 3 to 5 miles an hour? You cannot, it's not possible. Such laws are nonsensical, and yet somehow their effectiveness continues to never be questioned.

In the name of pedestrian *safety* pedestrian death rate was being increased.

That's life in our culture (for want of a lesser term). Odds and ends that are outrageously strange, perverted or even outright stupid happen and create serious moments – nodes, if you will – in the development of life as we experience it. Tributaries to "how the heck did we get here?"

Also, sometimes, extremely wonderful things happen. The ugly and stupid moments are more obvious, is all, but wonderful moments also happen.

Sometimes these things – events of note – can then be generalized into valuable lessons. Or even just quizzical anecdotes.

These can help one recognize patterns of justice and injustice, of brilliance and of idiocy... things that our society, this weird culture of ours, does. Sometimes I hear a news item and I can say, "*ah ha! I recognize that pattern!*" or maybe some celebrity is in court with some "sensational" trial and I know it will be very unlikely for this person to get a fair trial, because of the *Celebrity Rule*. Or I'll get news of some grievous twisting of the laws in one of America's more angry states and I know that either it's the *Too Many Lawyers Rule* or *the Mrs Grundy*

Rule, in operation here, frequently both[3]. Those two rules often interact and strengthen each other. Dang it.

Why is our world *that* way? Why are things the way they are? Mostly because *we* allowed them to become that way. We. All of us. You too. (But not me, of course. {That's sarcasm, by the way <so is this very statement>})

Note: some of these are called rules and some are called lessons. The difference is left as an exercise for the student; there is a logic to it. (Says so on the label.)

Now, let us have a look at some of these.

Except, not quite yet.

Concerning gender references: I use language the way it was intended, and not with any affront or judgment implied thereby. Trust me, if I want to insult someone, you won't have to look around for it – it'll be obvious. But why would I ever do that? We're all in the same boat, doing what we all *think* is best according to our own understandings, right? Any judgments or slurs you find in these tales lie entirely within your own perceptions, for none such are intended by me. OK, it's barely possible that shear accidents of language may occur and not have been noticed by any of the editors assisting me, but again it's really up to your perceptions to notice them, and up to your own emotional landscape to take offense or not. Therefore – as was stated in *the Hitchhiker's Guide to the Galaxy* – anything you still can't cope with is entirely your own problem[4].

---

[3]Also, sometimes just self-righteous stupidity, but we don't need to get into that.

[4]There are two problems with this whole "pronoun" thing America has going right now. First, you want to tell me what your pronouns are, why? So I can discuss you in the 3rd person not to-your-face? That's what pronouns are, how I might refer to you to someone else. How can that matter? Secondly, you really think it's OK to make it my burden to remember how to refer to you when you're not even around? I have a hard enough time remembering a person's name, which is far more

Adams' Laws

And the inevitable liability statement – my lawyers trying to keep your lawyers out of work[5]. To whit: please keep in mind that these are personal observations. My intention is not to denigrate anyone or cause any troubles out in the world. If any of these facts are wrong, then they are wrong. They are accurate to the best of my ability, but alas and alack, I'm still Human (in spite of life time of trying rise above that). Even if the facts that inspired the lessons or rules are wrong, I suspect that as teaching stories they are still valid. Truth is often like that. So are teaching tales. My intention is simply to offer some observations that have stuck in my mind. These rules (and lessons) came about while trying to understand this culture and people's behaviors within it, and also while trying to protect myself from what looked like various dangers, including predators, profiteers and the many funny-strange attitudes our world hangs on to with such energy.

In other words, these rules probably do not apply to you at all, nor to any one you know or have ever even heard of, and your mileage has already varied and may vary some more, and the contents of this book *may* be hot after heating. (Also, no user serviceable parts inside.)

In fact, skip this book. Don't risk it.

---

identity locked than a silly old pronoun. You want me to alter how I speak? Really? What hubris on your part! Or maybe I'm supposed to call you he / she / they / it to your face instead of by name? And the third (of two) problems with this pronoun craze, are you really just a pronoun? Do you *really* take your identify from a mere word? You might want to reconsider all that. Words have no power, save what *you* give them yourself.

[5]I have no lawyers. That's sarcasm. If you have a sense of humor, you'll have recognized it without it having to be explained. Otherwise, you might see offense where none was intended. Sarcasm is a powerful tool, but my experience says a certain percentage of folks will fail to recognize sarcasm for what it is. Maybe that should be another rule?

Still here? OK. Enjoy the book, or don't. Your Option[6].

~ Jeffrey

---

[6]This is a foot note. You may have noted I've already used some. I tend to use a lot of footnotes for side thoughts, jokes, back references and expansions on a thought that are not really part of that thought (in spite of how I just worded that). If you already knew that, then don't read this footnote, just all the others.

The Lessons

The 99.9% Rule

A common boast on cleaning products is that it kills 99.9% of all germs. The first time it occurred to me (at about age 11, maybe 12) what this actually means, I was horrified. Shocked, actually.

99.9%: That means 0.1% is immune to the stuff? One critter in a 1000 survives, to breed and fill in the population, a critter resistant to the whatever-it-was? This is very, very, *very* bad. This is the part that horrified a 12-year-old (or maybe 11) me.

Germs: define. This *must* be defined. Without a clear, precise definition of "germs" – which is a vague word at best – this statement has no actual meaning at all. All bacteria? All viruses? All prions? Algae? Fungi? Protozoans? Mites? Nematodes? Helminths[7]? Or only certain classes of each of these? There are billions of *types* of micro-critters that might be called "germs." You can't mean them all… can you?

Further: *how* does it kill? If it kills the severely tiny, isn't it then also toxic to cats, dogs, fish, birds, earthworms[8] and humans? And what about all those symbiotic critters? You know, the 30% of your body that is not actually "you" but is living there, contributing to your personal ecology and making it possible for you to be alive at all. Is it poisonous to those critters? I *need* those critters! In an absolutely antiseptic environment, life fails[9].

---

[7]What is a helminth? Well, actually, you probably don't want to know; let's just say "parasite."

[8]Without earthworms, it might be that life as we know it would come to a halt. Earthworms matter.

[9]This is one of the many yet-to-be-solved problems with long term life in space or on Luna or Mars: how to preserve and support the microbiome that makes possible life as know it. Life is all one Big Web, no one part of it is easy to separate from the whole.

Why do you think we now have so many *resistant strains* of undesirable critters – "germs", diseases, staff, TB, and so forth – now running around in our world? Incurable strains of things. It's that 0.1%.

Well, it's also the massive abuse of antibiotics. Antibiotics should have been very controlled decades ago, but instead they've been handed out like candy, sometimes literally just to shut up a patient with a cold, even though antibiotics can have no direct effect on a cold. A cold is a virus; antibiotics don't work on viruses. Nor can antibiotics make up for an immune system compromised by life style choices, couch-potato-ism, mainstream food, an over-stressed work environment, or overexposure to a fanatically negative news media!

First time I saw antibiotic hand soap on the consumer market I was horrified! Are you *trying* to kill us all off? For the doctors, OK. For the consumer? Hand sanitizer destroys all the complex natural ecology of your skin. Secondly, how about that 0.1% of whatever awful Bad Meanies might (and might not) be living there? All you're doing is making them *really* mad. Right there on your hands.

Constant use of antibiotic hand soap might (might) lead to dependence on that soap, since what you've really done is compromised your skin's ability to stay healthy on its own.

Maybe, maybe not. It should have been studied first. In great and thorough detail.

The *Blue Apple Laws* Law

There are a number of statutes on the books that do little more than demonstrate those making the rules today were the kids throwing spitballs at the ceiling during grade school science class.

Here's the story that defines *Blue Apple Laws*.

"Red," says some looking-for-public-approval politician, "is offensive to many people. Therefore, we are now outlawing Red Apples. From now on, all apples must be Blue. No one's offended by Blue."

Huh? That some one is offended by *reference* to a color might seem silly (and might not – ask the Washington Redskins – even though no human actually has red skin[10], all the same, some folks do identify that way), but really that's all in the ear of the listener. A person insults himself by reacting to what he hears, or what he doesn't[11]. But the point in this ludicrous scenario is the legislator responding nonsensically to a problem that actually needs no particular government attention.

Instead of leaving the problem alone – which is a government's best response almost all the time – they try doing something that is flatly impossible. Apples are yellow, red or green, but none are blue, and not even Monsanto can say otherwise. (Not yet, at least.)

This particular rule was invented when I noticed, several years ago, state after state in America passing pedestrian right of way laws. These laws state that cars must stop for pedestrians under certain conditions, sometimes under all conditions. Yet,

---

[10]Save in the case of a particularly bad sunburn. For those susceptible to sunburn.

[11]The basis of all "your mamma!" comments. It's the listener who offends himself, instead of laughing at an absurdity.

in state after state pedestrian deaths rates went up as a consequence.

Naturally. A fast moving, heavy vehicle has a minimum stopping distance. Under many conditions it simply *can not* stop in time for a pedestrian, especially one who takes his new right of way literally [12]. It's an impossible law. Yet the legislation doesn't notice that it's trying to rewrite physics.

It's not only a nonsensical law, but an impossible one. (Yeah, I said that already, but I don't want you to miss the point!) It's not always *possible* for a car to stop in time for a pedestrian. Worse, it does active damage. A law can not repeal nature, or physics. Blue Apple Laws are an exercise in stupidity.

Only the pedestrian can keep himself safe. Laws won't do it, especially impossible ones.

You can not outlaw high-school physics. Or even grade-school physics, as in "a body in motion tends to stay in motion." And a legislator whose mind was asleep during grade school science, tends to remain asleep while in office (The law of mental inertia, or is it political inertia?)

---

[12] I once personally witnessed a person step into a cross walk with fast moving cars only a few feet or so away. Squeals and smoking tires later, that person was *not* hit, thanks to talented driving. The pedestrian however appeared not to even notice his near death experience, failed to notice that he had put other people at risk, as other drivers might have been killed by that sudden stop. Thank you, right of way laws!

The Dancing Cigarette Box Rule

Yes, believe it or not, once upon a when, TV shows used such outrageous gimmicks as literal dancing cigarette boxes on a stage during a variety show. (Pictures are on the Internet.) Dancers dressed up as cigarette packages of the brand favored by the current sponsor of the show, of course.

Outrageous. Stupid. Insulting.

Or... was it clever, imaginative and intelligent?

(Keep in mind that, back then, no one really *believed* smoking was bad for you. The advertising even warred over which brand doctors thought was healthiest for you. Truly; would I make *that* up? Would anyone? Other than a cigarette manufacturer, I mean.)

Take your pick, either point of view is defensible, and that's not my point. My point is that it worked. Those dancing cigarette cartons sold more cigarettes, and gave further notion to the advertisers that they could control the content of a TV program, not just get the few minutes for whatever sort of advertising slogan / message / assault they were actually paying for. The commercial break was no longer sufficient.

Control of the actual content... nice. Power! Woo-Hoo!

And they're still doing it.

The family buys a certain brand of smart phone and suddenly everyone is in the living room with huge smiles on their faces sharing a great family moment together. So promises the ad. Yeah right... smart phones destroy family togetherness by encouraging solo time, lost in your games, your text messages, your whatever-you-found-on-the-Internet. Smart phones destroy sociability, and replace it with fake sociability – social media[13].

The problem is that y'all fall for this stuff. The dancing cigarette boxes win and they keep winning. You buy a smart phone because it will put smiles on your kids faces and maybe get them to spend a few minutes with you in the real world in a real moment of sharing. Maybe.

Worst part is, you probably don't even know that the smiling ad is what caused you to select that brand, because you didn't really pay close attention to the ad and/or you have no defenses against ads in the first place, because you've never questioned those dancing cigarette boxes, and those fake (and often feral) grins on the paid actors in them. Even celebrities doing commercials are *paid* to say what they say. It's really not an endorsement; it's a job. Dig?

Joseph Goebbels (Hitler's sadly brilliant propagandist) said it best:

> "If you tell a lie big enough and keep repeating it, people will eventually come to believe it. The lie can be maintained only for such time as the State can shield the people from the political, economic and/or military consequences of the lie. It thus becomes vitally important for the State to use all of its powers to repress dissent, for the truth is the mortal enemy of the lie, and thus by extension, the truth is the greatest enemy of the State."

You can replace "state" with corporation, or any other group of vested interest.

Unfortunately, for all of us, including even *them,* this statement has been adopted with enthusiasm and gusto by advertisers, corporations and politicians the world over. Though,

---

[13] Actually, more properly, anti-social media. At least at times.

in truth, it was hardly news when Goebbels said it. It's an old, old "wisdom" among power brokers and influence peddlers.

The hope in the first decades of television was that it would be a tool to uplift the Human Race, to provide continuing adult education, social instruction and genuine enlightenment to the masses. So was the first decade of the Internet thought by those who created it. In both cases, television and it's grandchild the Internet, this initial purpose and promise was suborned [great word, hardly ever get to use it] to mere greed and profit addiction.

Here's the short version:

Ads don't have to make sense to be effective. In fact, sometimes the more ridiculous, annoying and even insulting they are, the more you will succumb to the message, on all levels.

Here's a stumper: technically it's still illegal for an ad to lie about the product. Let's take just one, rather minor example. Yamaha stereo amplifiers are known to be misleading on their ads and spec sheets about the actual amount of power they put out. They are *known* for this. Yet no one has made them correct this issue. (Is it a true issue? Is it a false "knowing?" Maybe it's a lie put out by the competition. Many possibilities here.)

Another one: Microsoft has actually said online that they have no bugs in their software. Fortunately for them, few believe this. Yet they said it. (Or perhaps that spokesperson was not an official voice? Again, who can say what's true? But I *do* know that they have bugs, hundreds of thousands of bugs. I *know* this. So there [as they say]. Trust me. [Ha!])

Here's another one: a package of shelled sunflower seeds that dares to actually say "gluten free." Yes, that's a true statement. It also has no rat poison in it, but I don't see that advertised. Sunflower seeds have no gluten. Never will, never have, never can. Putting it on the label is a true statement that becomes a false one by implying that other brands of sunflower seed might have gluten in them, or any product that does not proclaim itself gluten free might have gluten in it. Extremely misleading and predatory. But not illegal. (Leveraging the consumer's ignorance instead of correcting it is always predatory, always short-sighted and counter-productive.)

Many, many false claims in ads. They get away with it sometimes because the exact statement made says one thing to the lawyers, another to the designers of the product yet something completely else to the consumer. So challenge them on it and they'll explain the technical meaning of the phrase and then they're covered. Dang it.

Or it's even a true statement: "contains no rat poison!"

For example: Apple Corporation *still* says, "we don't get viruses." Well... that *is* a true statement, but only from the technical definition of a computer virus. To the consumer it says something else entirely and is not true to *that* understanding. Yet there it is. Legal, technically.

The consumer uses the term "virus" to cover anything that goes wrong on a computer (that, and "hack" which the public also does not really understand). In fact, virus is just one of many types of malware. Malware, PUPs and PUAs[14], viruses, trojan horses, back doors, spy ware, and a 100 other nebulous and uninformative (to the uninitiated) terms.

This has the extremely bad side-effect of leaving millions of Apple product users with the false belief that they are immune to all malware. Very bad on Apple's part. Very.

OK, that about sums up the Dancing Cigarette Box. But let me recap anyway:

Advertising is not your friend. In *almost* all cases the ad will be misleading, pandering, sloppy with the facts, misleading

---

[14]PUPs are potentially unwanted programs and PUAs are potentially unwanted apps – which is in no way different from PUPs, as apps and programs are exactly the same thing. Any idea that they are different is just marketing again. Like the term "cloud" which is just a repackaging of "Internet" so they can get you to buy the white album yet again -- see, in fact, The White Album Lesson

(did I say that yet?) and predatory. Advertising is a very, very sophisticated art, involving group psychology, herd dominance and herb subservience, sexual innuendo (even buried sometimes in children's ads) and many other forms of blatant manipulation.

Even shorter version: advertising will usually try to *compel* you rather than convince you. They compel you by manipulation. To convince you, they'd have to actually have a demonstrably good product and then appeal to you intelligence. More work, lower profit and (mostly) more work!

Fortunately for them they've managed to educate you out of almost all of your intelligence and self-awareness. Good for them!

Quit being a Sheeple, dang it!

The Death by Convenience Rule
or, The Running Water Lesson

Used to be, in the old, old, old days of years gone by that no one had running water in his palace, home, shack or hovel. You brought water in (or in the case of a palace, had it brought in) as needed, sometimes from far away.

A scene from M*A*S*H: "You carry water a full mile? How can you do that?" asks the naive but brilliant American surgeon in Korea. "That's where the water is," says that dazzling, intelligent and educated-in-Paris native woman.

So here's the story that epitomizes the *Death by Convenience*[15] concept: once water was far away and you were extremely careful in its use. The farther you had to carry it, the more cautious you were with its use. Ah, but now the water pump is in your own yard, because you dug a nice well (at great physical labor, perhaps with the help several people). So you don't have to be *as* careful. But sometimes it's raining outside, or it's dark and or it's cold. It's still not really convenient. So you move the well inside, under the kitchen and put the pump right there. Now water is available anytime you want it.

Except you have to pump it. And also that certainly didn't work well for large ranches with many mouths that want watering. So the water tower is invented. And then whole townships adopt them and start running massive systems of

---

[15] Which could also be called the Death by Automation Rule. See Frank Herbert's entire series Dune, all six books.

pipes and plumbing to every residence, and now we have running water. Wow.

And now, instead of being cautious with it, you use water freely. You leave the sink running while you shave. You take a 20-minute shower instead of a five minute one, or a one hour bath that would still use a lot less water. Last estimates, the average American wastes (WASTES!) 30 gallons of water a day. That's almost 10 *billion* gallons of water a day across the nation, *wasted*.

And then folks wonder why we're having severe water issues in many parts of the country now. Well... not *all* of us wonder why.

But it sure is convenient! Ain't it?

There are entire townships in America where the water table is totally depleted, water has to be trucked in.

Even that is way too convenient, frankly, as it tells the people that no matter what some one in authority will take care of it for me. Death by convenience. There it is.

Let's generalize this now. Automation and marketing constantly push "convenience" to the consumer, and every new "convenience" serves quietly and subtly (sometimes not so subtly) to weaken the general public. Hand held calculators destroyed people's basic ability with arithmetic. When's the last time you saw a checkout clerk make the change without looking at it on the cash register first?

In fact, "convenience" is a primary target for new marketing. Anything that makes life more convenience is a marketable product, right?

What? You can't count? You need the machine to tell you what the change from $18.23 on a $20 bill is? Well, yes; many of us do now. That's really very bad. (For one thing, how does the consumer know if he's getting the correct change? He doesn't, that's how.) During a power failure, many stores can no longer function at all anymore, even cash only. They've forgotten how to take cash and make change, or even how to add up a shopping cart of goods!

Electricity is a *HUGE* convenience, and consequently a huge vulnerability should it suddenly go away. Far too many *human* skills have been replaced with mysterious and magical "technology." If any of it went away, most folks would not be able to survive. *Literally.*

Of course, not all convenience is to be avoided or even looked askance at. Some things truly just save time. But let's keep that extremely thin line of balance in mind. Don't let automation take away your abilities, your mind, your body or your freedom.

Can you walk away from all technology and get along without it? If no, then you're vulnerable, and weakened. You ability to survive is called in to question. And so also your ability to rise above and be everyday more than you were before.

Consider this: one week without electricity. What do you do?

[panic mode on...]

OK, now that you're in a bad panic – at that simple and quite possible scenario – let's suggest something much easier. One day a week, do without your toys. Make it a regular thing; one day a week. No computers, no cell phones, no TV, no washer / dryer, no microwave. Even keep the lights in your house to a bare minimum. You know, close to how Humans have lived for nearly all their considerable history, how most of us lived until just after World War II. You'll still have heat, you'll still have some light. You'll still have access to emergency services. But you also now have access to yourself in ways that perhaps you haven't even thought about in far too long a time.

One day a week. Can't do it? That would be a serious addiction, wouldn't it? You really want all those *conveniences* to control you? That's what addictions do, you know.

Still... Your option. Always.

The For-Profit-Only Rule

There's a problem with the 21st Century.

"Just one?" asks the cynic in the room. Well, no, obviously not just one, but one specifically I want to point out right now. And it's a *major* one.

When I was a kid (yeah, yeah, back when Cheops's pyramid was still running behind schedule) the teaching was that the purpose of a business is to provide a service for which you receive a reasonable profit. Today, the teaching is that the purpose of business is to make a profit.

Huh?

What happened to "Service"? What happened to "Reasonable"?

Kind of like what happened to the Hippocratic Oath all doctors are reputed to take most solemnly. It's been modified several times over the centuries, gradually making it OK to put money and personal convenience ahead of the profession of Healer. (OK, that was the short version, and *perhaps* not entirely fair. Toughies.) In fact, doctors are really not healers any more, but technicians of the Allopathic System. "Allopathic" as in the AMA, CDC and WHO, and what those organizations often think is the only way to do things.

(Fortunately there are other system of healing. And, yes, even allopathic has its uses – saved *my* life at least twice, but it's scarcely a complete approach to health. Even Dr Welby[16] was a vastly better Healer than are too many doctors today, but that's getting off the track).

For profit only… The moment you go for profit only, the moment that becomes your focus, you are not in business any

---

[16] Old medical TV show, a kindly elder gentleman of profound insight on every illness that came his way. The "Dr House" of his era, in a sense, but not nearly as arrogant!

more. At least not with your alleged product. The only company for whom profit actually is the product would be an investment firm. Banks can offer profit as a side-line or a come-on product, such as that amazing 0.5% they [dare to] offer on savings account now. [Piffle... go back to the 8% interest rate we used to get on savings accounts, guys!]

For profit only... means you are not in service to your customers, but at most to your investors instead and your upper food chain (the CEO, CFO, VPs of this-and-that, and so on).

How do you think Bill Gates got to be so very, very rich? By focusing on money? No. Emphatically no. He got that way by focusing on his product and his vision. He had a vision to bring technology to the entire planet. And he did that. Sometimes ruthlessly, but always in alignment with his ultimate vision: helping everyone on the planet. Did he let the investors and stock holders drive the company? No way, dude! He made the decisions and in doing so he made more millionaires than J. P. Getty did, which was another one of his goals[17].

Bill Gates gets accused of a lot of petty and nonsensical stuff, but truly one of his goals was to make more millionaires than had ever been made by one person before. How is that petty? PLUS... he did it by *not* focusing on the money, but by focusing on the products his company was creating, by focusing on service to the planet.

Unfortunately, Microsoft is no long under his control and it is devolving very fast. Well, more of that under *The Microsoft Rule*.

Further, when a company, especially a major company, is focused on profit only, they are actively damaging the fabric of society. OK, that takes some explaining.

---

[17] That is, this particular goal was to spread the wealth around. He did not set out to be one of the richest people in the world. That was side-effect of keeping his priorities straight, plus being in the right place at the right time.

Profit. Did you know that in America a publicly held company is *required* by law to do everything possible to maximize profit or those in charge can go to jail? Major argument against taking a company public.

Profit. So you get the market saturation with your product, and sales are starting to drop. What do you do? One thing you can do is cut the quality so that the life span of the Thingoid (our hypothetical company makes many great *Thingoids*) is reduced. There's a small lag, while the good ones gradually wear out, but now the shorter-life-span units are getting out there and sales are again on the increase.

Profit. Now the sales begin to level out again, albeit at a new higher level, but profits must always be increasing, right? (Huh? We won't get into what's wrong with *that* here, not enough space in this article.) So, now we create another Thingoid almost like the first one, but this one's New and Improved! Wahoo! Sales go up again.

Profit. Now sales level again, and maybe even slump a little because your public found out the new product wasn't any different than the old one. So now we start a miseducation campaign that tells our customers that every person in their household needs two or even three of these. And we'll further add on a service contract, annual subscription.

Profit. That's better. How to advance it now? Well... let's reduce the documentation, while making it prettier, but less informative. Now calls to tech support go up, but we'll farm out the tech support to an independent company and charge a percentage of their take for doing so.

Profit. That one didn't get us as much an improvement as it should have. So we'll switch the entire product line to an annual new model. A new model every year, with a great dog-and-pony show to convince the investors that it really is something new and improved. Convince the investors and – Hey! – our stock value just went up.

And so it goes. We started with a product, maybe it was even a good one. Now we're hoodwinking our customers just to keeping raising the amount of profit. Our Customers! The ones who gave us all that money, the ones who support us with their loyalty! We've scammed them, faked-and-taked them, and worse yet... we like it. We think we did our job, and did it well.

Profit. A steady profit is not considered good enough anymore. The amount of the profit must keep increasing. The *rate at which it is increasing* must keep increasing! That's addiction, by the way.

Worldwide, there is a phenomenon going on among all the big companies and even a lot of the smaller ones: profit addiction.

The problem with addiction is
1. you'll do anything to get your next hit
2. the hit has to keep increasingly
3. you can't quit, the addiction warps your mind and thinking and you might not even know you're hooked, and probably don't care even if it does occur to you – now and then.

Gosh.

What's the point of this rule? Knowing that this is the big thing that drives nearly all companies and enterprises[18] now you can shield yourself against fake products, fake updates, pointless updates, fake improvements. Stop feeding their addiction. You'll be doing them a favor in the long run.

It gets subtle though. Do you have monies invested with an investment firm? They will in turn put that money in to companies that perhaps should not be supported.

OK. So do the best you can. Even the Big Companies are into the Scam for Profit phase of their devolution now. And it is devolution. In the long run, any company that turns its focus to profit only is doomed. It maybe take a while, because of the size of the thing, but it happens.

---

[18]Bravo! To those of you

By the way, did you notice that recently Microsoft laid off 1900 employees? And Windows as an operating system is down to 72%[19] of the market, where it once was over 95%.

Yet they were able to spend *$100B* in the last three years acquiring other companies, much to the distress of the fans of those other companies. Like when Disney bought Star Wars and there was a world-wide "disturbance in the force."

Companies eating companies eating companies... Why would they do that?

Profit.

---

[19]As of the time of this writing, per "reputable" on-line sources

The Ford Pinto Lesson

This lesson is a thoroughly disgusting one. And a very important one to be aware of, so you can guard again it.

Back in the 1970s Ford had a wonderful little run-about called the Ford Pinto. They even had a special bicentennial version of it, all decked out red, white and blue. There was a problem with it though. If rear-ended the gas tank could explode, just like in a Hollywood action movie. Cars don't normally do that – that's really "just" a Hollywood thing (mostly). Except for the Ford Pinto.

So a law suit was brought against Ford for their exploding gas tank. Kind of proper. I'm not a big fan of law suits, ultimately *everyone* loses, but sometimes a law suit is the only feedback a big company will listen to. Unfortunately.

During the course of the trial it came out – during the testimony of a [I believe] former Ford engineer, that the problem with the gas tank was known before hand, but management decided that it would be cheaper to suffer a law suit than to issue a recall. The cost was balanced, and they set aside $10 million for the expected law suits (approximately – this is all from memory).

The jury was properly horrified. The press was all over it. Blah, blah, blah. And what happened? When the verdict came in against Ford the judge awarded *precisely* the amount of money that Ford had set aside for the law suit. Even with the testimony that it was calculated in cold blood. Instead of hitting them for 10x or 100x that very amount, the judge awarded the precise amount that was allotted. The lives risked by Ford's manage team of the time were thereby given a monetary value, and though technically the court ruled against them, Ford won. The trial came out precisely as it was supposed to.

The value of lives knowingly placed at risk had been given a price.

Ford won. That's the bottom line there.

So what's the lesson? Maybe it's "if you're big enough, you can always get away with it." Maybe it's "life is cheaper than ethics." More likely it's: watch out for yourself, because you can not count on the Big Guys doing it for you.

I'm not saying all companies behave this way, nor am I even saying Ford behaves this way, then, now or ever. (Could have been just a specific executive, long ago retired; maybe that engineer even lied about the cover up. Who can say, especially now?) But stuff happens and ultimately, it's up to each of us to keep ourselves safe, as best as we are able.

The Forest Gump Rule

A friend of mine often cringes when I accuse so-and-so (person, or corporation) of being "stupid." Truly, she's quite correct. Accuse people of being stupid and eventually that's all you see.

However... (ah yes, "however") as *Forest Gump* said so very well, "stupid is as stupid does." Meaning that – stupid, smart, or otherwise – what was *done* was a very stupid thing. That person or company *did* stupid. Sometimes it takes a really smart person to do a *really* stupid thing, oddly enough.

Some examples of doing stupid (in no particular order, folks!)

1. Monsanto with its genetically modified products. Such as, what's commonly called Franken-wheat, whether that's a fair assessment or not. There's a serious *potential* problem with genetic engineering at this stage of the art. I'm not spouting unfounded conspiracy nonsense here, but real science. However, the argument is outside the scope of this document. (Sounds like a fake argument when put that way, doesn't it? Oh well. I'll direct to you an article of mine on the subject, one of these days.) Especially when one of the engineering "improvements" was to make wheat that produces sterile grains, so that the farmer must buy his seeds from Monsanto next year and cannot simply save some of his harvest for replanting. This is a risky thing to do. Very. What unknown side-effects or changes to the wheat berry (which is where flour and a HUGE percentage of our processed food products come from) might come from forcing the seed to into sterility? (OK, this might be old data. I haven't tracked Monsanto in a while, but I do know that at one time, at least, this was indeed one of their "improvements.") Secondly, what happens if Monsanto isn't able to deliver fertile seed for that next crop, for some reason? Bad, very bad.

2. Round-up. OK... very controversial. Many folks say it's wonderful. Many folks say it's evil or even a plot to eliminate the excess population (a la Scrooge, no doubt). Well, here's a fact: since farmers started heavily spraying their wheat fields one week prior to harvest, the incidence of wheat intolerance, crone's disease and other digestive or allergic conditions has gone up massively. OK (again)... correlation is not (necessarily) causation, but at the very least it needs serious investigation, yes? Serious investigation, not investigation geared to favor a multi-billion-dollar industry, but one that favors public health and safety. In truth, many other nations (not the U.S.) have outlawed Round-Up for this and other reasons. Again, this needs serious examination – anything else would be "doing stupid."

3. On the flip side, DDT. Huh? Isn't that one clear-cut? Well, not so much. That case needs to be reopened. Turns out that DDT *may* have been given a bad rap by one (I believe just one) over-zealous person who got it in his head that DDT was very bad. Poisonous. In fact, there is now evidence suggesting that it was fairly benign, in its side-effects. Perhaps far less evil than Round-Up and other such chemicals now saturating the global food supply. Needs to be reexamined. Anything else would be "doing stupid."

4. LSD – generally considered a very bad street drug. Hallucinogenic, no redeeming value. Turns out (yes, once again) that's not the complete story. LSD was specifically invented by a psychologist to help schizophrenics. Which is does. Can (*can*, I say) turn a schizophrenic into a normal person (or more normal). But The Law decided to make it illegal after running away with anti-drug sentiment taken all out of proportion. Well, just recently some of these facts have "surfaced" (as they say – in fact, these facts were never buried, just roundly ignored) and LSD has been opened up in some jurisdictions for medicinal use. Which is what it was always intended for. So there was a cure, or at least a treatment, for some serious conditions that was made illegal. A lot of pain, crime and insanity might have been alleviated by examining the facts instead of relying on prejudgments.

5. Marijuana – another drug unfairly treated. Yes, it's a drug. But... it's also a naturally occurring plant. Here's the kicker: Humans are born with cannabis neuro-receptors already in their bodies. *Born with them.* Caffeine, nicotine and other drugs cause the Human body to develop receptors, which is part of the addiction cycle, but we are *born* with cannabis receptors already in place. That speaks a lot right there, it does. The Human body seems to want it. In fact, now that the laws have relaxed in many places, it is coming out (but just like the data on LSD, these facts were never really not known, just fashionably ignored) that Marijuana has a great many very serious medicinal benefits, which I won't get in to here, as it's beside the point. What is the point? Simply outlawing the stuff was a reaction to a perceived threat and not a rational decision. Perhaps it should have been outlawed, but the reasons given for doing so were never born up by the facts. That is what made it "doing stupid."

6. Cyclamates – Here's a very, *very* sad case. Back in the 60s cyclamates were decided to cause cancer and were banned. They were replaced with saccharine. Some years later it came clear that saccharine causes cancer and that the studies on cyclamates were faulty. Did they reverse the situation? No. They continued to leave cyclamates illegal and all that happened to saccharine was that grocery stores were required (for a while) to post signs saying this store sells products containing saccharine. So we (our legislators and the public who blithely trust the legislators, in spite of evidence that we shouldn't always) sentenced a lot of people to being overweight and a lot of other people to cancer. And we did nothing about it. (By the way, recent studies [as of this writing] suggest strongly that *all* sugar substitutes are now implicated in the various dementia and neuro-degenerative conditions, which have been on the rapid rise since the (coincidental?) release of Aspartame on to the market. Tell you what: how about just give up *sweet* as a craving?)

7. The DARE Program – first, I am NOT saying (NOT) that DARE is/was a stupid program. However... I read the official report filed after DARE's first year. It was an analysis of how the program had done. Simple, reasonably clean report. The conclusion was horrifying, however. Turned out that drug use in the "target group" (grade school children between certain ages) had gone up 400% during that year. (I do not recall any analysis of how those numbers were achieved, which would have been a serious failure in the report, by the way, if not included.) The conclusion – the horrifying conclusion – was that DARE, *therefore*, need additional funding. A program that probably achieved the opposite of its avowed purpose should be increased? Not terminated or reexamined from scratch? Clearly something was seriously wrong there (I can make guesses about it – anyone with a smattering of child psychology could, too – as could most parents) but no recommendations that DARE be totally restructured, reexamined, the approach reconsidered... just increase the funding. What a blatantly self-serving conclusion (concussion?) Who sponsored that program? Who sponsored the report? Truly, how *dare* they?

8. America's Food Supply – Back in the 1950s and 60s, "fat people[20]" were extremely rare, and often from a medical or psychological condition. Look back at some Jackie Gleason movies or TV shows. He was considered hugely overweight. Massively overweight. He was probably all of 240 pounds. By current standards that's hardly overweight at all. Morbidly obese, yes, but not unusual today. Why is that? How did 300

---

[20]To use a term no longer considered politically correct – but the "political correctness" is itself highly offensive to some folks, so either way, someone's offended! Might as well use the term less likely to be misunderstood. No judgments implied. "Fat" was simply the term then, and not always an abrasive one. Ask Minnesota Fats, the famous pool player, for instance.

and 400 pounds get to be so common it doesn't even draw special attention? The rise in obesity *coincides* with the release of NutraSweet (marketing name for aspartame). Of course, it coincides with lots of other things, too, so, can't say there's a causal relationship there [21]. Just pointing out a correlation. Further, America's food supply since that time (even before that) has been increasingly denatured, increasingly processed, increasingly filled with funny chemicals and artificial this-and-that's. The "food" on the market is often non-nutritive, lacking in essential minerals and vitamins, and containing questionable substances, left and right (as the saying goes.) This is a complex topic and way beyond the scope of this article. Let's just say that the current food supply in America is perhaps the best example of all of doing stupid.

Stupid is as Stupid Does.

Our society, our so-called culture, does "Stupid" extremely well, sometimes. We excel at it, even.

Gosh.

---

[21] Although, in fact, anomalous weight gain – as it's called – is one of the top 10 side-effects of this sugar substitute, according to many studies.

The Fortune Cookie Rule

This one's more of an observation about Human psychology, at least as it expresses itself in our truly strange culture.

Everyone knows what a fortune cookie is. (If you don't, where've you been hiding out? I'll join you.) In fact, "fortune cookie" is a phrase sometimes used to discount something, as in "oh, that's just fortune cookie saying" or "he spoke in non-stop fortune cookies."

As in what fortune cookies have to say might be amusing but of no actual value to anyone, anywhere.

Sorry, senator, that turns out not the be the case.

You read a fortune cookie and you see something possibly profound, but mostly obvious and you just go yeah-yeah, gimme the lottery numbers, never mind the fortune cookie wisdom. (There's another derogatory use of the concept!)

But maybe you remember what it said. And maybe years later (or even minutes later) something happens in your life and a light bulb goes off over your head and suddenly you get it! Bang! Wow, even.

Now, suddenly it's not just a fortune cookie, it's *real* wisdom. And you get it.

The point? You didn't get it until you got it for yourself. It was just a silly saying on a tiny slip of paper wrapped up inside a pretty bad excuse for a cookie. (OK, some of you like those cookies... you have my official permission to call yourselves weird.)

The question: why is that?

1. Because we're prejudiced into the idea that fortune cookies are "just for fun" and nothing serious?

2. Is it because in our culture we're taught to resist education and learning from others' experience?

3. Or is it just normal Human psychology, Human behavior?

4. Or, the inevitable alternative in nearly all cases, something else?

Just keep in mind that those bits of wisdom you encounter (in cookies and other places) are invitations to learn something the easy way. You can take the Universe up on the offer or not.

Learn it the easy way, or learn if the hard way.

Your option. Always.

The Good-for-Two-Years Rule

The computer industry got started the hard way, and perhaps the only way possible. Computers, to get to their present state, needed millions of engineer-hours of development and experimentation to become the almost useful gadgets they are now (never mind, not going to explain that just now).

Trillions of dollars spent developing the things. Trillions. Where'd that money come from? Not from governments (though some of it certainly did). Not from private funds. Not from any research grant. All research grants put together can't equal the amount of money spent on developing computers in the last 55 years.

So where'd it come from?

From the consumer. From you, that is. Who kept believing the sales ads and kept buying equipment barely able to do what it was advertised to do (yes, it could, but not well). And the development cycle was very, very fast so that often within 12 – 24 months of having bought that expensive and delicate piece of equipment it's actually obsolete. Not really, but marketing pressure sure made it seem so. So you went out bought the next extremely expensive version of the equipment.

Gradually it did get better, more useful. Because *you* were funding the development. (Well, possibly not you-you, the you reading this document, but… well, you get the idea.)

And the development cycle was fast enough with enough legitimate improvements that it was worth putting out that kind of money on a regular basis. The equipment was mostly amortized over two years anyway (sometimes) and that helped with the expense.

But starting around 2000 (or 2004), consumer grade computers were finally able to do just about everything a typical consumer might want to do. (When tablets came out it demonstrated that actually the computer was already doing more than the typical consumer really wanted – a simpler device was just fine. Hence the unexpected success of the tablet.) This meant there really wasn't any longer any justifiable 2-year buy-it-again cycle really going on. Companies adapted by doing things like annual subscriptions to tech services and upgrade / support services. By coming out with a new version of the hardware every year (e.g., Apple's cell phone line... "new and improved" every year, and getting increasingly skinny on the improvements, which mostly are not improvements at all, but just some reorganizing of the furniture and the cans on the shelf).

But those mega-corporations that grew up during the boom years of the computer industry were hooked (addicted) to massive profits all the time, always going up. Now the market was effectively saturated. They adapted, as I said, in limited ways, buy the real way they keep it all going is by continuing the invoke the 2-year rule.

I see a lot of people who say, "oh my computer is soooo old" when it turns out it's only 4 or 5 years old. That's programming! You, not the computer! That's manipulation of the Herd. (Go! Go! [Baa-aaa-aah!])

Today, a desktop computer bought now should last 20 years, with possible repairs or upgrades (desktops can be repaired and upgraded quite easily). A new laptop today *should* last about 12 – 15 years, only it won't. The quality of laptops has suffered greatly in the last few years. So a laptop bought maybe 10 years ago is going to still be useful (assuming good health and no artificial sweeteners in its coffee) about the same length of time as brand new laptop bought today. Go figure...

(By the way, that's one of the ways of continuing to increase profit, as I mentioned in the For Profit Only Rule.)

Another thing holding the 2-year rule in place is the investors. Start-up companies (and there are still quite a few, every year) need investors to bootstrap the operation. Investors want to see a return on their investment in 18 months, more or (preferably) less. So a two-year cycle works quite well there, too. (See "The Investor Rule" for more on that one.)

What's the point here? Don't believe the ads and the culture and your friends who maybe "drank the cool aid" about when a product / device / gadget is old. This includes houses, cars and many other things as well. Our business-driven culture relies on frequent sales and many of those companies will do anything to get you to keep on buying.

This is one reason why the Great Masses remain also the Great Poor. The Great Corporations keep milking them. Greatly.

As the old saying goes, "the rich are rich because they spend like they're poor, while the poor are poor because they spend like they're rich." But that's the programming, of course, the advertising.

Don't fall for it. Keep you own eyes open. Look at the product in front of you. Does it still work? If it's having problems then take it an expert, one with enough experience to know if it *really* can't be fixed up and does in fact need to be replaced. Laptops, especially, need periodic maintenance, because of the extremely toxic (to a computer) environment they are constantly subjected to: the Internet.

All your stuff should last a very, very long time. If it didn't, it was either very badly made or you fell for some fake advertising, either way, don't buy from that company again.

Your choice. Only the consumer – that YOU bub! – can make the corporations honest again, by failing to support their dishonesty.

The Investor Rule

Investors are important, especially to a startup company. It is said that the American patent office was started expressly to give folks a way to invest in new products. Investors make things happen, though it's the inventors who provide the things to be made to happen. (Of course, ultimately, it's the consumer who really pays for the development of a product, as well as for any legal ramifications, law suits, liabilities, insurance… all the "expenses" our strange society might put a "deep pocket" to while bringing a product to market.

Investors. Sometimes an investor loses his money. That's the risk, and why profits when an investment is successful are justified.

Sometimes, though investors don't like it when they lose their money and they take it to court. And sometimes that case does go to the investor. But it's often like trying to get blood from a turnip – if the company failed, there's nothing to sue.

And sometimes a company is "failed" on purpose so that its assets can be bought up by another interest at 10 cents (or less) on the dollar, thus defrauding the investors and contractors of their rightful due. Certain well known "business folks" have made a life long practice of such things.

If you're an investor, *be* an investor and accept that it's always a risk. Sometimes it will pay off, sometimes it will not. That's that the reality.

But here's one serious way in which investors are abused, and it's become such a "normal and expected" thing that folks don't see it for what it is.

Companies, especially start-ups, give the investors way too much power, way too much decision and influence ability.

Investors are usually not experts in the field in which they are investing. (If they are, it's a wholly different matter, but then why aren't they doing their own start up if that's the case?) And they are subject to all sorts of misinformation, cultural memes [the true meaning of "meme" not the Internet's meaning of it] and so forth, so that it's almost inevitable that they will only hold the product down, or even ruin it.

Example, in the computer industry, especially in Silicon Valley (as it's called) it is common for a start up to bring the investors through now and then, pointing out all the "young people" they have working for them. Apparently there's some sort of misunderstanding that only young folks in computers can come up with new and innovative ideas. Nothing could be farther from the truth.

A master programmer takes a good 18 years of 60 hours a week *after college* to become a master at his craft. (This was per one of the founders of a major software firm, back in the 90s, and it certainly matches my own experience.) But the emphasis on "youth" means the executives don't want any "old" people around for the investors to see. So now we have reached a point in the computer industry where some actually believe (believe, I say!) that 35 is now too old to be a programmer. Meaning, in those companies at least, there are no master programmers any more. This is a self-defeating piece of social nonsense, started by the computer industry and now maintained by the investor culture itself, who wholly believes it by now. Phooey, I say!

Let's all drink the cool aid, yep indeedy.

This goes a long to explaining the current serious problems with quality that the computer industry has (and often doesn't even seem to be aware that they have – I mean, with no master programmers around, who's going to tell them that product What's-It is just plain terrible?).

No master programmers. Because of a misunderstanding and very bad choice on how to market to investors. Very bad, indeed. Repercussions it will be very difficult to ever get rid of.

What's the core of this lesson? Invite your investors, wine them, dine them, party them, listen to them even, but *never* let them make your critical decisions, appearances not withstanding. They are investing in *you.* So be what they are investing in, in the best way you know how to be.

They have their expectations, sometimes even around appearances (suits, age, whatever), and it may have nothing to do with your reality. To honor their investment and their risk, you have to follow your *own* best judgment at all times. Anything else and you have abused the trust the investors gave you.

Any company that cow-tows to the investors has lost its way.

By the way, investors includes stock holders. [That's the punch line, in case you weren't sure.]

(Another way to generalize this rule is to simply say never compromise your own judgment, especially when it goes against what you thoroughly believe to be correct. [On the other hand, one needs to always be open to additional data – one *might* be wrong, of course.])

The IQ 85 Rule

I live rurally, mostly. Small towns. The hustle and bustle of the city lost its appeal, especially when it turned into 90 decibels and more of constant chaotic sound, polluted air, heavy crime, toxic foods and a very weird culture. (Otherwise, big cities are just fine… [yeah, that's sarcasm].)

Small towns appeal to me far more. Oddly enough, in spite of the hype by Big Cities, rural communities are far from being backward. In fact, they often have some very extraordinary people living in them, for many the same reasons as I do.

So some years ago I had reason to visit "the big city" (big compared to where I was living at the time, at least), and was seeing some things with a fresh eye, as they say. On that particular day I was fairly stunned by what I was seeing. Ads, billboards, marquis displays, with misspellings, lack of grammar, sentence fragments, use of symbols that meant nothing to me[22], slogans that clearly said something far from what was (probably?) intended… the light bulb suddenly went off over my head and it occurred to me that all this advertising and "shout outs" were designed (perhaps knowingly) to hit an IQ around 85.

OK, from a marketing point of view, it's a defensible tactic: your advertising is understandable to more people that way. Especially in America where the average IQ – as measured against the rest of the world – hits about 95. (Meaning, as one movie pointed out quite humorously, half the people you meet really below average intelligence, only even more so in America. Geez...)

---

[22]Brand logos, apparently. Between texting and brand logos and such, our language is rapidly changing from an alphabet based one to a pictographic one, with a subsequent lowering of data and clarity as a result. Oh well.

However, as the misspellings and vague grammar and accidental multiple meanings embedded in the ads and slogans suggested, this is ultimately a self-defeating tactic.

This sets a minimum bar for literacy and critical thinking (aka, self-defensive thinking). The problem with such a lowered standard is that too many people will never even try to rise above it. This is sufficient to let them buy that new pair of shoes they saw advertised last night, and that's sufficient for the needs of government and business alike.

Aiming all that flotsam and jetsam to a point "below average" will inevitably have the effect of reducing the average literacy and powers of thought. Just as signs on every street corner, on every curve and bump on a highway make all signs simply that much harder to notice. Sign saturation denatures the effect of all signage. (Should mention that one under "Stupid Is As Stupid Does.")[23]

So another generation grows up exposed to this constant, impactful noise (auditory or visual, it's still noise) and that lowered standard for reading and observation now becomes the normal level, which means – here it comes – you have to lower the standard yet again, in order to keep that small group on the left-hand side of the bell chart (the below average bunch) within the reach of your marketing.

Aiming all of it at a low intelligence level, ends up lowering the intelligence of the Herd in general. And this has been going on Big Time in America for at least the last 75 years.

Not that advertising has ever been wholly wonderful and uplifting, though it might have been.

By the way, another important point of this phenomenon, is that you are automatically excluding all those folks to the right of "normal" on the bell chart. Your advertising will fail on

---

[23] There was also the 60s song that sang "signs, signs, everywhere the signs, do this, don't do that, can't you read the signs?" We're so far beyond that point now…

the intelligent and especially on the wary, those who have built up a defense against advertising for purposes of simple survival.

Because advertising is so traditionally predatory, misleading and dysinformative, many folks out there have indeed built-up defenses against it. (I suggest you all do that, then advertising would have to change and half the problem would be gone, just like that!)

When your advertising goes on for years and decades, constantly misleading, constantly misstated... portions of the Herd develop a sense of distrust and suspicion against all advertising.

And that's just stupid... (get it?)

The *It's illegal* Rule

This one is simple and (maybe) short.
You *never* control a thing by making it illegal. Make a thing illegal and you've given up all control over it.
Oh, you say, but law enforcement then becomes responsible for controlling it. They can handle it!
Really? Then why is it that so much of the drugs and other "evidence" seized by law enforcement ends up simply disappearing out of the evidence room? This is a nation-wide problem, and in fact world-wide problem. Sometimes known drug dealers get completely off because *all* the evidence disappeared. (Maybe they paid to have that happen? Who can say?)
Also, if law enforcement works, how come street drugs are worth many billions of dollars a year?
OK, maybe a bad example. (And maybe not.)
Here's the meat of the rule. When you make a thing illegal, cocaine, say. You give up all control over it. Over the quality of it. Over the toxicity of it. Over the distribution of it. Over the taxation of it. Over the education around it (all education on illegal substances necessarily goes not much further than "it's illegal"). Bad cocaine then kills people. Medical expenses go up for everyone, because of those so poisoned. Billions of dollars are exchanged every year in America alone over cocaine and there's no tax revenue on it. Not that that's an argument in favor of legalizing it (though it would be some, I expect).
OK, even "good" cocaine kills people. But with it's being illegal you have no control over distribution, dosages, quality, real public education about it or how much a person can consume. And there's no chance of producing a less dangerous version of that product, then, is there?
I am NOT advocating making cocaine legal. It's a stupid substance, damaging in so very many ways. But I am

suggesting that making it illegal does not, has not and cannot solve the problem.
Doesn't. Can't. Never will.
We need another solution. That applies to *any* situation folks might think needs controlling. Drugs, guns, movies, porn, sex education, public demonstrations[24], sit-ins, laugh-ins (OK, not laugh-ins) everything. Make it illegal and all you've done is to create a *huge* black market and removed all consumer safeties. Now it's a money-making venture.

What's a "black market?" One that's outside of all government control and government taxation. (Hmm, doesn't sound bad when put that way. Or does it? Oh well.)

Find another way to deal with it. "Illegal" just doesn't cut it any more. Maybe never did.

---

[24]Yeah, some people seem to think that public demonstrations need controlling. They are controlled – they're LEGAL according to the U.S. Constitution, the People's right to assembly. It is legal, therefore it is controlled.

The 5G Lesson

Recently America installed an upgrade to its Internet and cell phone service backbone. This was called 5G, as opposed to 4G and 3G and even 2G that came before.

This is a massive improvement in "bandwidth" for "devices."

Definitions (might matter, so there)

Bandwidth: in the digital age, means how much data can be carried moment by moment on a given channel or data outlet, such as your Internet connection (high-speed vs normal service, say). Moving data faster requires more "bandwidth" or what's simply, commonly called "faster service." Bully...

Device: for some reason the computer industry has never taught its operating systems (Windows, iOS, Android, etc) to recognize what sort of gadget it is running on, so instead of referring to "your phone" or "your laptop" they – all of them – say "your device." There is no technical reason for this (as a *very* long time programmer, I know this) and I have to assume it's simple laziness on their part. (For Shame!) Or possibly it's a marketing device (ha!) of some kind.

We'll ignore *device* (now that I have that particular pontification off my chest) and focus on bandwidth, because that's the justification or reason for 5G.

More and more the computer industry wants people keeping their backups on cloud storage, such as cloud drives like Google Drive or Microsoft's One Drive and 1000 others. Why? Partially because it really is simpler for most users, but mostly because it represents *massive* passive income for the computer industry. The downside is that it requires the ability to move a LOT of data around on the Internet, preferably always fast, fast, fast. (See the article on Death by Convenience, here.)

Further, people are increasingly isolated into their little virtual worlds: laptops, phones, etc, doing their own thing, even in the same house, 5 people might be doing 5 entirely different things: watching movies, playing on-line games, texting to 12 other people around the planet who also doing the same thing. Those 5 people might not interact with each other, right there in their own home, for hours at a time. (The "babysitter" that was once simply TV is now a fully automated entertainment vending machine called the Internet. Again: bully.)

All this wants massive amounts of data moving around the word as fast as possible, or faster.

OK. 5G represents a significant upgrade in bandwidth. Huge, in fact.

Excellent, as they say. Wonderful! Get it out there, get it set up and sell it all over the place! And, by the way, be sure to fully retire 3G now, so that we force all those sluggards still using their older phones off the network... (why? There was nothing wrong with those phones or that service. And maintaining 3G would in no way have interfered with 5G. Maybe because it temporarily bumped up cell phone sales and was justifiable buried inside the 5G "upgrade." That's the only reason I been able to come up with. Give me another, anyone?)

Get it set up now. Sell it now. And we'll sell more cloud storage, and more streaming and everyone in the house can maybe start using two devices at once! Also, faster service means we can charge more for it. Yippee! WA-Hoo!

Yeah, yeah. The Knute Rockne school of sales. Ra! Ra! (Whoopee-do, even.)

But there's a problem. *Maybe*[25].

5G also represents a very, very significant increase in the amount of energy being shoved through the air. All transmissions, all wireless connections, even your wireless mouse, need radio signals of one type or another, cast through the air. In small doses there are no problems with this (that we know of). But we are 60 years past the point of "small doses."

---

[25]Actually, evidence is growing to support that there really is a problem

And now, in the last 10 years or so, the amount of energy being bled into the air has more than tripled. Quadrupled, perhaps. Maybe more.

So? So what?

Well, besides the fact that this is necessarily heating the air (this is, after all, many gigawatts of electricity being fed directly into the air, you know... energy! Power! Solar cells, windmills, diesel generations, nuclear plants [which are really just sophisticated steam engines, did you know that?] and all the rest. Power! Poof, gone into the air! Heated air. Oh goody) ... besides all that, there have been for over 60 years many (times many) studies demonstrating conclusively that EMF (electromotive force, if you like, or electromagnetic field, or several other things) and RFI (radio frequency *interference*... go figure) or EMR (electromagnetic radiation) and all that (whatever term you wish to put on it) have a profound effect on mammalian nervous systems. Either way, that includes you. You are a mammal, like it or not. But it also has been shown to affect even basic cellular metabolism all across the ecosphere, not just for mammals. It's also been shown to interfere with migration patterns in birds, breeding cycles in insects and many other things.

Human sleep cycles, too.

60 years these studies have been around. At least. Well, OK... yes? So?

So... many people and many organizations raised massive objections to 5G's going in, at least without further testing. The studies demonstrating that there may indeed be a serious health hazard are legion. I know of no study concluding that there is no health risk. Such would be hard to justify at this point anyway. Yet all this information, all these objections and petitions were roundly ignored.

Why? When looking at the facts, one can only conclude that money trumped public safety. Of course, that's when looking at the facts, and we might also say that the legislators heard neither the facts nor the protests, and were ignorant of all this outcry against further gigawatts of energy being boiled into the air.

Perhaps the legislators don't even realize that that's what it means, all this wireless tech. In which case one can wonder if they should be in their offices. Are not public offices jobs, with job requirements like any other? Should they not have to qualify for the position even before going up for election? I would think a major decision maker for 320 million people would need a whole heck of a lot of qualifications… but apparently the Great Masses disagree with me. Or perhaps they've never considered that a high office (of any sort) is really just a job, an especially heavy and demanding one. (But that's another article for another book, I reckon.)

(Given some of the folks elected to office in the last 40 years, one can in fact be certain that few have ever considered the requirements for high office. Oh well.)

OK, this isn't really a thesis on 5G (or political theory). It's a Life Lesson. What's the lesson? (Or is this a rule? Figured out the difference yet?)

Profits will trump potential health issues, even wide spread ones. The greater the profits, the more public health and safety will be ignored.

Another, way of putting might be to say vested interest doesn't want to hear facts that disagree with its agenda. (Basic Human psychology, by the way, at least in our culture.)

"I can make millions on this! Don't contaminate me with facts. I don't want to hear them." Aw, heck.

Take your pick on which way to summarize the "5G Lesson"

(Humans… I get the feeling there's a reason why the Great Galactic Council hasn't yet contacted Earth Descended [26] Humans and invited them join the community. You think?)

---

[26] "Earth Descended" Humans is a term that was used by Fred Saberhagen in some of this science fiction. It was to differentiate against the possibility that other humans might exist in the Universe as well.

The Louis, Lewis [Loo'eeeee] Lesson

Americans are funny. (In so many ways, but so are the rest of you, so there.) They manage to mispronounce so many things.

Billet Doux becomes 'billee doo" (Instead of "bi'lay do")

Boise become "boy'zee" or "boy'see" depending on whether you're a native or not. It's actually "bwahz." In fact, "la bwahz vee(y)" would be the proper pronunciation. It was French, like billet doux. It's legal name, in fact, is La Boise Ville" ... go figure.

(Except on some government documents it actually is referred to as "City of Boise City." On that you might want to review the *IQ 85 Rule*. It applies to governments too.)

But one that really bothers me is Louis vs Lewis.

Louis is "loo'wee"

Lewis is "loo'iss"

That all there is to it. (Deal with it.)

In grade school, back east, 4th grade I was taught quite firmly (obviously, if I still remember it) that only "ignorant people" would call say "Saint Loo'iss." Yet I soon found that "everyone" calls it just that, and perhaps no one ever says "Saint Loo'ee."

Except me? Well, I generally try to avoid it altogether. I'd sound either stupid, ignorant or snobbish by pronouncing it "correctly" so I try to say nothing at all. St Who?

We might even mention "Ragg Mopp" here. An old song with the refrain, "r a g g m o p p, rag mop! doodley-do!" Etc. That song when it was out and new caused a stir among educators all over the nation, because their students were now spelling rag and mop incorrectly, since the song said so.

What's the point here? It's a subtle one, but I can sum it up simply: society and societal norms can force people in to certain behaviors, whether correct or not, sane or not, important or not. Societal norms, in other words, can hide information, hide data, even hide truth, under "normal and expected" or "everyone else does it" and such things. (Worse, societal norms can even enforce neurotic or psychotic behaviors as "normal," but best not to even mention that here.)

Beware what the Herd does and what "everyone knows."

Beware of "everyone knows" anyway… even if you never visit St What-ever-its-name-is.

The MCI Lesson

Back in the late 90s MCI – a communications company – was caught with its fingers (whole hand, actually) in the cookie jar. I won't get into blame here, that was all taken care of back then (sort of). Short version: the bills they were sending out to customers (some? all?) often had extra charges in them. $0.55 here, and $1.05 there. Those bills were highly itemized, and a month's bill might go on for several pages. An extra entry here and there would almost certainly go unnoticed.

Except it didn't go unnoticed forever. They eventually got caught. They had raked in millions of dollars they never actually earned.

Well, investigations, fines, etc, and it was taken care of, right?

Not so much, really. More damage than the obvious was done. By making this public it also grabbed the attention of many a company worldwide that one could do things like bill padding on a very large scale quite successfully. The trick was not to get caught.

"Hmm," said all the other corporations. "How can *we* do that, and not get caught?"

That damage is not so easy to fix.

Unfortunately, it's easy to not get caught. One way is to simply stop itemizing the bill. (Which eventually they all of them did.)

Another possibility, today, with the heavy automation layer (aka, the Internet and "the cloud" and commercial "cloud services") is to say simply (whenever a customer inquires about any billing irregularity) "oh yeah, we've been having trouble with that software" or another popular one "well, you know there's like three separate systems the billing has to go through and sometimes it gets confused," or some such statement, and they reverse the charge and all's well. (Humph.)

Under such a system, a wide spread bill padding scheme would never even get noticed.

An "honest" mistake and no on can prosecute them. The transactions are all so buried any more in that self-same automation layer than it's nearly impossible to know if your bill is being padded an extra buck or two.

Normal business practice. You might review the "For Profit Only Rule" at this point.

It's an addiction. Cheating customers is one way to get your fix. (If your market is saturated – in business-speak – then that might be the only way left open to you, especially if you don't understand how to create new products or otherwise expand your product line. See the New and Improved Trap, on that one, and the Pacled Rule as well.)

By the way, I'm not accusing anybody of such practices. Just suggesting that it's possible. It's even possible that the entire "MCI" thing mentioned above never happened. Or might be hot after heating.

The New & Improved Rule

New and Improved? Wahoo! Gimme 12 of 'em!!

Or not...

Before the computer industry changed consumer expectations around new and improved (because for a while, maybe 20 years, new and improved mostly meant exactly that when it came to computers) new and improved was a joke to most people. It was rarely taken seriously. Well, some folks took it at surface value and that's why it kept being used. Sometimes that claim worked.

Then the computer industry hit, making the consumer pay for the development of a consumer grade computer that can actually be of some use to the typical citizen[27]. So every year, or six months or even 18 months, something really, truly was better about the equipment and/or the software, usually both[28]. Now significant updates are rare, mostly just dog-and-pony shows[29]. There are occasional improvements now, but they tend to be years apart.

Yet the new and improved dance goes on.

Here's the problem: it's a trap, for the manufacturer, as well as for the consumer, who already has the Pavlovian ring in his nose. Ring the bell, and the consumer buys something. Gah!

---

[27] By the way, the original founders of modern computing, say circa 1940s more or less, would be glazed and dazed and amazed that a computer (a COMPUTER) could possibly have become a consumer appliance with every day use. They never imagined such a thing was possible, even though they made it possible.

[28] And keep in mind that this was before the Internet, so software updates were distributed physically, on disk. You actually got something *in your hand* for your money.

[29] Absolutely nothing significant about Windows 11, for instance.

Here's one specific. It has to do with Windows and Microsoft, but this is hardly the only such example. There are many times many of these going on.

Windows XP was just about perfect. It ran fast. It did what most people needed and did it with style. Certainly with more style than any version of Windows since. Yet it was retired, after Big Bill quit running things. The problem with it was that people were hanging on to it, even with Vista and Windows 8 out there, many folks were content with XP. So, XP was retired, forcibly. So Microsoft got a few new sales again and some CEOs / CFOs were able to keep their jobs for a while longer. (Yeah, that's cynical. So?)

(Did you know that there are *still* occasional updates for XP? And a significant number of the ATM's in America run are still running on XP. Think about that one. One of the reasons presented for retiring XP was that it wasn't – and couldn't be made – secure. Yet here's a piece of banking still running on it. Hmm… as the sage said.)

But no version of Windows since has worked as well as XP did. All they *needed* to do was to upgrade the core a little, add a few security gates and call it a new version. They didn't do that. The next versions were all dogs compared to XP. Windows 11 is a complete joke, as you can see if you look up reactions to it on the Internet. (And that's sugar-coating it, if you want to know.)

I recently had a chance to run an old, old (yes, really old) computer with XP on it, right up against one with Windows 10 on a brand new, leading-edge desktop with all the high-power accessories. Fact is, the old and ancient XP machine could do many things faster than the "new and improved" rig could, even with its high-power hardware. That, on an old, slow, sluggish computer. I'd like to see XP on a new, fast leading-edge machine, but unfortunately it's pretty much impossible to get XP to work on anything new now. (They rigged it that way.)

Of course, if you switch your hardware over to Linux (Ubuntu, say) you again get those wonderful speeds like XP used to have. Which increasing numbers of folks are discovering even as I write this. Linux's market share is increasing. (Windows is down to around 70% of the market, down from more than 95%.) Here's the kicker on that: **Linux is free**.

But Microsoft's stock value keeps going up, so you'll never convince them they're doing it wrong. Like I said in the "For Profit Only" article, though, once a company sacrifices quality for profit, they're on their way out. It might take years yet, but Microsoft is noticeably losing market share already.

Imagine how fast Windows could be if they'd maintained the quality of the product instead of counting on faster computers to make up for their laziness (or incompetence)? Fast and beyond fast. And that could have added so very much to productivity all over the world. *All over the world*, I say.

What a shame.

The problem, of course, was that if Microsoft had ever stopped coming out with "significant new versions" their sales would have plummeted. Or at least the profits would have quit going up, up, up. (Personally, I see nothing wrong with just keeping a healthy but stable level of profit. So I only cleared a billion dollars last year, why does mean I have to clear two billion this year? But that's why I've been called a bad business person, right?)

If Microsoft said, "XP does it all! We're done!" they might have had to close their doors. Or maybe they could have focused on some of that 6-figure bug list they have. Improved quality, instead of the profit margin. The odd thing is that if they'd focused on improving the quality their profit levels would have gone up anyway. (As the pirate the false eye in *Pirates* said, "that's what I can ironic.")

I have an inside source at M$FT that tells me (truthfully? Maybe. Probably) that programmers there are mostly of the under-educated sort, with just a handful of higher-end programmers who are overworked and highly stress out. Also he tells me that programmers are told to NOT work on bugs. They work on new features only. You want to work on bugs? Do it on your own time, apparently is the message. (I suspect the bugs that do get worked on are the ones specifically trounced upon by the Big Clients, and not the ones that inconvenience the Little People.)

Sort of like the "It's illegal rule", by denying the extent of their bug list they lose control over it and over the quality of the product. All their products.

In short they are betraying their customers, their employees and (most importantly, from *their* point of view) their investors and stock holders, because as a software company they are on the way out, unless they can clean up their act in a hurry.

However, probably the stock holders have little to worry about (unless they consider the ethics of supporting a dishonest company), as Microsoft is rapidly becoming more of a holding company than a software manufacturer. So... it's OK.

Right?

New and Improved is a trap. When your product is perfect, admit it. When it's not perfect, admit it. And move on as appropriate. There would always have been more work for Microsoft to do as a leader in software design. Too bad they gave up software. But alas and alack... (as the bard said).

Why is Microsoft spending more money on accumulating other companies than they are on fixing the many (legion, even) problems with their mission-critical-to-the-world products? I don't know, but it looks like they've given up the software business. Or maybe they can't keep feeding their profit *addiction* by "doing it right" ... so they think.

Marketeers of the last two or three centuries (at least) created the "new and improved" concept; the computer industry then leveraged it to such an extent that it's now seen as a Truth of the Universe and even a requirement for all right thinking people (it's not), so it's up to them (Marketeers, that is) to fix this criminal and disastrous situation. Except they won't, 'cause their stock values keep going up, so they fail to see a problem, and that's *your* fault. The consumer's fault, that is, and the stock holder's fault. You. Keep rewarding them and they have every reason to think they are doing it correctly.

Stop being Sheeple and the companies won't be able to get away with all that garbage any more. Stop validating the companies (all of them) that put profit ahead of quality, that put the stock holders ahead of the consumer[30].

Proper business puts the consumer first, the employees second, the stockholders third and the management tree last. Last. And guess what? Your profits will go up. *Always.* (Well, you also need an occasional burst in creative insight thrown into the mix now and then, and a service-orientation toward your customers, but that's easy enough when you hire the right people or educated your employees correctly – educate, not program.)

Now, that said, let's check today's stock values…

---

[30] Or the CEOs ahead of the employees. But that's a different form of slow-death for corporations, and we won't go into that here. Probably won't even mention it, here. So there.

The OS11 / Win 11 Lesson

An odd thing happened a couple years ago. Microsoft, who had said Windows 10 would be "the last version" (they'd just keep updating it) and Apple with OSX (OS "10") which *they* said would be their last version both went to "11" with in a couple months of each other.

More suspiciously even yet both companies suddenly require (*require!*) a special chip on the computer to even run on that machine, a chip whose use is supposedly optional. So why does it have to be there if I'm not even going to use it?

After Microsoft moved to Windows 11, Apple quickly moved to OS 12 and now on to OS 14… guess they couldn't stand having the same version number as Microsoft – maybe… who knows? But once the version "10" (OSX) barrier was broken, they haven't lost any time moving forward with the numbers. Marketing, of course. A different generation's take on how to do it. (Maybe)

Microsoft's Windows 11 is not doing well. The company itself has said reception to Windows 11 "has been disappointing." Well… who (besides them) was actually surprised? Windows 11 has not one single new feature in it that's worth a dang. What it mostly has is a new "softer appearance" – their words. Really? It's a computer… I hardly care what color anything is. It's not a fashion accessory. It's a *computer*.

But that's beside the point. Both companies went to a "security" chip at the same time, both of them breaking previous marketing statements in doing so. It's just plain weird.

I'm not going to spin conspiracy theories here, as there's really no data to do so, other than what's already been stated[31].

So far at least, under Windows, use of the TPM chip is optional. Or supposed to be. But we are so far past the point of knowing what's really going on inside these machines that saying it's optional does not mean it isn't used by the OS anyway. On this I have no data, but that's the problem, isn't it?

(By the way, the "TPM" chip is "trusted platform module" – personally, whenever something on a computer calls itself "trusted" I get very suspicious. It is, ostensibly, a security chip, adding some kind of security storage to all consumer machines. And, by the way, Linux, though it will support the TPM, does NOT require the chip. So why do Apple and Microsoft? (Especially Apple as OS-what-ever-it-is-now is based on Linux). There... that's as far along the lines of conspiracy as I'll go, lest some men in black suits show up at my door... maybe with a flashy thing.)

The sort version is this: when something unexpected and largely inexplicable happens, be suspicious. When it comes at you simultaneously from two or different directions, be *very* suspicious. That does not mean get paranoid about it, just note it, and move on. That's all.

(When a thing fails to make sense, take note!)

---

[31] I *could* mention here, though, that any company that reverses previous statements or promises without sufficient justification is not a company that can be trusted, any more. They broke their word, dig?

The *Spirit of St Louis* Lesson

And here you might start by reviewing the *Louis, Lewis* article. Just a thought. As I write this, I'll be saying Louis to myself, and you'll be reading it as Lewis. So right away we're not really communicating, are we? (Sort of. Maybe)

There was a truly awesome movie many years back about a truly awesome event: Charles Lindbergh making the first nonstop flight from New York to Paris. It was historic and younger people today might have a hard time understanding how exciting and wondrous it really was. Suddenly those two continents were only hours away (30 hours, maybe) and not a week or more away from each other, by ocean ship.

It was awesome. Take my word for it. Or watch the movie with Jimmy Stewart, *The Spirit of St Loo'ee.*

(OK, I won't do that again, especially as even in that movie they say "Saint Loo'iss." Bah.)

Why is that a lesson though? Because Mr Lindbergh had to work like the Dickens (as they say) to get funding for the plane and the flight. There was huge cash prize waiting for the first person or team to make that flight, yet getting a bank or investment firm to offer up sufficient funds (about 1/10th of the prize money) was very difficult.

No bank was going to do it. Well, finally one did, and they did it because they believed in the pilot, not so much in the adventure, itself.

What's the short version here? Sometimes seeming reckless adventurers are not actually so reckless. Sometimes they are absolutely necessary and they will go out of their way with great energy to overcome all obstacles that the normal public will put in their way. At great risk, with great energy, they force society into the new and wonderful whatevers that it really needs. Kicking and screaming they bring us forward and give us exactly what we need, and even what we want, but were too nervous / cautious / conservative / afraid to do ourselves.

Geez...

Thanks, Mr Lindbergh for forcing the Banks into a tiny risk and starting the massively profitable Aerospace Industry. Kicking and screaming, did you drag them into a big new era.

The Stupid Geniuses Rule

There's a funny thing about really, really smart people. They are the only ones capable of doing really, really stupid things.

Ordinary people could never have come up with the A-bomb, or with genetically modified crops before we really know enough about genetics to ensure they are safe, or with that utterly ridiculous web of treaties and alliances that caused World War I to happen[32], or...

Ordinary people can get along quite well, though they wouldn't have cities or over population or refined poppies (cocaine, heroine, meth), or polluting and oxygen consuming cars or even steam engines. The ordinary person would still be living the way ordinary people have always lived, for at least the last 250,000 years (oldest known *Homo sapiens sapiens*, 250K years – oldest known recognizable human of any type, about 3.5 *million* years. And archaeology is still progressing).

Ordinary people would still be living in a world without global warming, without an eroding ozone layer, without high blood pressure or wide-spread morbid obesity or any of 1000 different kinds of addiction. Also, without antibiotics or a thousand other ways of fixing the things we used to die from.

But the extraordinary people, that 1/10 of 1% of the population at any given time have always been there. They are the ones who create all the stuff the Ordinary People come to accept and to use, even to take for granted, even when they utterly fail to understand the thing. Even something as simple as radio is over the heads of most people, let along the hyper-complex inner workings of a computer. (Heck, even most so-

---

[32]If interested, read the Barbara Tuchman's *The Guns of August.* Pulitzer-prize winning book

called computer programmers can't tell you why a computer does what it does, not any more at least.)

To the Ordinary Person the works of the Extraordinary is just Magic. (Or Magick, if you prefer.)

Well... all that is OK. Maybe. Arguably anyway. (There are those who say we shouldn't have done all this "progress stuff," and even, as Douglas Adams pointed out, maybe coming down out of the trees wasn't even such a great idea. This isn't my point, here, though.)

What is the point, you ask? (Thank you for asking.) Well, I'll tell you.

There also the problem that Extraordinary and Extraordinarily Creative people don't always fully appreciate the long term impact of what they would do. And sometimes not even a truly Smart Person *can* actually foresee all the consequences.

When the transistor was invented at Bell Labs, 23 Dec 1947, did they have any idea that it would lead to cell phones, satellites and space-based weapons? Cruise missiles, lethal drones, remote viewing cameras and robot military dogs on sentry duty?

(And about those robot dogs now in use by the military – no, that's not sci-fi, not any longer – didn't *anybody* watch the Terminator?)

Were all these good ideas? Does it mean the transistor should never have been invented? Probably not. Should the inventors of the transistor (Walter Brattain, John Bardeen and William Shockley, later known for further work in semiconductors such as with the Shockley Diode and such) have known this would make satellite weaponry and robot guard dogs possible? Absolutely not. Well, maybe not *absolutely*, but where the technology went after the transistor came along has been totally extraordinary and quite beyond any rational reckoning beforehand.

OK... that's nice. Where's the *really stupid* part of what really smart people do?

All over the place, really. Take another example.

How about all the 100s of studies indicating that aspartame (the artificial sweetener) is dangerous to *everyone* and yet the substance is still legal and even widely used in America? Is that smart? The first week aspartame was out several 100 people died (the ones who could not tolerate phenylalanine, one of the three toxic substances it breaks down into in the body – the other two are less dramatic). The response from the FDA was "we double checked, no, it's safe." Really smart… really stupid.

Or how about all the lawyers who twist the law into forwarding their own agendas into "winning at any cost?" (See Keanu Reeves in *the Devil's Advocate* for more on that one[33]). They violate the intent of law by twisting the letter of the law, and the letter of the law can *never* fulfill its intent. Language is like that; it's always and only an approximation of the real communication. Along come those particular lawyers who love twist and pervert the word in order "to win" … thereby ensuring that we all lose. Them too. For the Law ("Law" not "law") was meant to bind society together into a mutually supportive whole. These intensely clever folks do this amazingly stupid thing of playing fast and loose with the law, thereby weakening the ties that bind us. Ah well.

I could go on. So could you! You've probably already thought of some examples of your own.

But I think the point's been made.

Really, really stupid things come about by really, really smart people doing things and leaving them in the hands of the ordinary person. Who doesn't understand the limitations, the hazards. The guy driving that Big Bad Diesel Guzzling Track doesn't know that he's shortening his own life with diesel fumes, poisoning the environment around him, including his own home, damaging his and others' ears with the excessive noise, and a hundred other little bits of long-term damage to the world he

---

[33] *"I'm a lawyer! I win! That's what I do!"* he said, speaking to his boss, actually the Devil, as it turned out.

lives on. He doesn't know any of that. Nor does he care, probably. What he knows is that he loves his truck, he loves the noise and the feeling of power. He doesn't know the psychology of such things nor is he even slightly embarrassed by what his love of that truck tells others about him. He just drives it. Not in the least embarrassed. Silly person.

But he didn't invent it. Smart People did that. Smart People who didn't think it through (to be kind, one *hopes* they didn't think it through). Smart People who create stuff and turn it over to other folks who fail even worse to understand the ramifications.

Why does this observation / lesson / rule matter? Maybe it doesn't. But it is interesting to realize that many of the problems of the Human Race right now have been brought about Super Smart Creative folks doing things that were exploited by Super Business Types, neither of which thought about whether the whatever-it-is *should* be manufactured, published or otherwise made known.

(Though, many of the creators of the so-called AI [34] software are now touring hot and heavy everywhere trying to get folks to understand that it's extremely dangerous. Yeah it is, but the problem is it's already out the gate, and the smell of profits is in the noses of all those CEOs, with their own Pavlovian nose rings... dang it.)

Double edged: without its Smart People, the Human race would die out. But with its Smart People, it might die out anyway, just in creative ways... unless large numbers[35] grow a superlative sense of responsibility, and do that pretty soon.

---

[34]"So-called" because it's not "AI" in the traditional sense. It's MI – machine intelligence, at most. Possibly not even that. Real AI is definitely a thing to be cautious of, but the shortest statement of it is that this is really just a (very) fancy database lookup, pulling data from the entire Internet, so (therefore, even) very little of what it says should be taken at face value. The Internet is a soup of misinformation.

[35]Actually, it only takes 10% of the general population to make a massive change. Think about that!

(We could all of us stand to develop a sense of ethics and personal responsibility, but our "modern society" isn't big on individuals doing that, is it? Ha! Fool 'em and do it anyway!!)

The Hill House Rule

There was a truly marvelous movie, made in the finest of Gothic horror tradition, around 1963. A truly scary movie, without any blood, gore, wildly tense music, 3D effects or CGI. *The Haunting*. As in the *Haunting of Hill House*, from the marvelous story by Shirley Jackson.

What made it awesome was the fact of fantastic special effects (long before CGI, those effects were all done the hard way, basically they are exactly what they look like) and (and!) the fact that they never showed the monster behind the door. You never actually saw the monster. So it left your imagination utterly free to rise to its own level of pure terror.

Stephen King in his awesome non-fiction book *Dance Macabre* made good use of this, pointing out that that was *precisely* what made that movie so successful, so scary and so iconic.

Here's the irony though.

In 1999 they did a remake of the movie, and totally blew it! They took *the* movie that was the icon of a truly scary movie – never show the monster behind the door – commented on by one of America's foremost horror writers (fantastic literary writer, by the way, *Stand by Me*, *Dolores Claiborne* and *Shawshank Redemption* also to his credit) -- and yet they *showed the monster behind the door!*

Gah!

This is really very ironic.

And it says much about Hollywood and it's mentality. Producers get worried about a movie failing. They pay no attention to aesthetics or to proper story telling. They worry only about the profit. Which is why so many really bad movies get made every year. They're too cautious with too little understanding of how to tell a really good story and no courage to take a risk anyway.

The Hill House Rule[36] says that even the greatest example of How to Do It might get ignored, even by a good cast and crew.

The remake had some serious people in it, including Liam Neesan, Catherine Zeta Jones, Owen Wilson [whom I think was miscast in the part actually, though he did quite well, of course; he's a good actor, but his personality just didn't fit], among others.

So now *the Haunting* is an icon both of a serious success *and* a serious failure.

Not that the remake flopped, not at the box office, but as a story and as an event in the history of storytelling, it most certainly was a flop. Movie cost $80M (?!) to make and grossed $180M at the box, so I suspect the investors have no idea at all that they sponsored an *aesthetic* failure.

---

[36]As opposed to *Cider House Rules*, I guess.

The Mrs Grundy Rule

In the TV show *Gunsmoke* (very popular at the time, iconic, really, still in reruns on some small, local stations) there was an occasional character known as Mrs Grundy. In fact, this character goes back to at least 1798 and the play by Thomas Morton *Speed of the Plough*.

I won't make you read the play, I'll just tell you. Mrs Grundy is an archetypal character, the keeper of the public morals, an extremely conventional and priggish person who is a willing tyrant for conventional propriety.

Which way too often is neither conventional nor proper. Go figure.

She's the constant busy body, the constant gossip and spreader of "you know what so-and-so did" rumors. Given a chance she will tattle tale on everyone she can. She considers it her personal mission and a truly righteous thing to do.

We all know a person like this. At least one, maybe more. Unfortunately.

But here's the problem with Mrs Grundy. She's a sneak, a peeping Tom and probably the worst pervert in any given community, since to suspect people of doing improper things she must herself be an expert on what improper things look like and how people doing them behave.

Mrs Grundy is the very pervert she's supposedly trying to prevent!

Ironic, huh?

Beware of those who wish to control other people's behaviors, or who place judgments on others with very little real information about those people. (The court of public opinion is profoundly guilty of doing just that. There's a little Mrs Grundy in all of us, dang it.)

Beware of the keepers of the public morals. (In another book I'll detail why morals in general are dangerous, in our culture as it stands. It's a counter-intuitive argument, which is why even mentioning it right now might be a bad idea. So, I won't mention it here. Or did I already? Dang.)

A true innocent can't possibly even imagine the things that Mrs Grundy is constantly expecting (hoping?) to catch us all doing.

All the way back to 1798 such a person was characterized in a stage play. Well, we can be sure that such people go all the way back even to Babylon and Assyria. And earlier.

Perhaps well-meaning, the Mrs Grundies of the world do incalculable damage. They get publications removed from the shelves because of a single word, perhaps. They put fig leaves on blocks of stone carved in certain likenesses (never getting that the Bible tells us that it was only after losing innocence that Adam and Eve grew self-conscious and shy… doesn't that tell you something?). "She" fails to see the beauty inherent in the work just as it. And that's the real damage of a Mrs Grundy: she denies and destroys all beauty that she fails to understand, denies any higher aesthetic and wants to control the behavior and freedoms of all other people. Ambitious, that is!

By the way; this has nothing to do with gender. This personality type comes in male and female both, and any other flavor you might entertain. It is gender neutral. More importantly, one wonders how many Mrs Grundies have become judges and lawyers.

Or worse – legislators. Maybe in Texas, working to reverse individual rights in the name of a petty and angry righteousness. ("We look for things, things that offend us." -- see the Pacled Rule)

Gah!

Mrs Grundy! Mind your own dang business! (You pervert, you!)

The Odysseus Lesson

We had a very disappointing moment in the continuing halfhearted conquest of the Moon just recently. A privately build lander, named Odysseus, jointly managed with NASA, successfully landed on the Moon and then ... gosh ... fell over on its side.

The landing base was too narrow! Did the designers of this otherwise wonderful piece of hardware never even look at the LEM, NASA's lunar lander from back in the 60s? A 1960s piece of technology worked better than 2024 piece of tech? Really?

It was an obvious error, too. First time I saw even a mock-up of the thing, my instant reaction was "top heavy, unstable." It looked like a phone booth with narrow struts on it. Sadly, I was right, and however-many aerospace engineers – all probably too young to have watched the original moon landings – were wrong, dang it. (Double Dog Dang it, even!)

So this rule is very simple, really. Odysseus simply is the latest example.

When you've only got one chance to do it right, you need to make triple sure that it *is* right. Check with other experts. Double-check your math (or the modern engineering equivalent of engineering math... watch the movie *Apollo 13* for an example of the kind of arithmetic it took to get us to the moon, on slide rules and computers less powerful than a handheld calculator 10 years later).

Check it. Check it again. Avoid the embarrassment.

The original LEM had a really wide base on its landing struts. That was an obvious clue. How could modern engineers *possibly* have missed that one?

And yet, it was still able to do perform some of its mission. Thank you, Odysseus! You did some of your work in spite of us silly creatures.

For want a nail a horse was lost
For want of a horse a rider was lost
For want of a rider a message was lost
For want of a message battle was lost
For want of a battle a war was lost
For want of a war a kingdom was lost.

(to quote Shakespeare…)

A few bucks more for longer / wider struts. For want of a nail. Oh well.

(Think Tardis[37] falling over on its side. Ugly and silly scenario that would be!)

---

[37] For those who don't recognize the reference, it's Dr Who's strange transport device, forever (apparently) stuck looking like an ordinary "police call box," which is a very definite British concept, and that's fine, for so is the Doctor!

The "Pacled" Rule

"We look for things. Things that make us go."
~ The Pacleds, in their first encounter with the Star Ship Enterprise

Star Trek, the Next Generation introduced an interesting new alien race in one of their episodes: the Pacleds. (say "pack-lids"). [Borg Species 95012, by the way – no, I'm not a Trekkie.] They are a sort of interstellar moron roaming around out in space, stealing technology from other races where ever they can. They were trying to coerce some cool stuff from off the Enterprise. Including the Chief Engineer. Big mistake, that.

Interestingly, you occasionally see a Pacled wondering around on the space station in the later series DS9, set some years after this first, contentious encounter. So everyone survived this first dramatic moment, but at the time...

Here's the thing that struck me about the Pacleds. They were able to operate the technology they had acquired from various races, but they never understood any of it. It was "way over their heads." All magic black-boxes to them.

This made them very aggressive (success with aggression reinforces it as a successful tactic), and also extremely dangerous. To themselves as much as to those they attacked. This was demonstrated in the way the Enterprise defeated the Pacleds, with a total voodoo lie the Pacleds were too "stupid" to spot as a lie.

When you operate a technology you do not understand, you risk becoming a Pacled. We look for things, things that entertain us. Things that make us money. Things that make us go.

Getting used to operating tech not within your understanding is – potentially at least – a very dangerous trap.

Eventually you can't operate it and you can't repair it[38]. Maybe you can't even tell if it's really broken.

Oh no! You say. Not true, you say. There's always an expert around. No, not really. The computer industry itself has become a great example of a dwindling understanding of tech. Repair technicians often can't spot how to fix some very simple problems. "Tech Support" speaks in strong accents and follows very abbreviated check lists, without any understanding of why the check list is as it is, but managing to charge you a lot of money with outright lies about how and why it's not working and things you've just got to have.

Just like the Enterprise did, though in their case it was justifiable, to get Geordi back abroad. But...

Don't be a Pacled. *Understand* what you are doing. At least try to.

---

[38]See the original Star Trek pilot, in fact. Those aliens could no longer repair the machines left by their ancestors. Oh well… so much for smart.

The Ad Backfire Rule or, Modern Four-Walling

There is a "three strikes" rule in law, which says three convictions and you are put away forever. Yeah, right. That works, sure it does... especially for the tax payer. (Prison was supposed to be corrective. Many states even call their system this-and-that department of *corrections*. How is keeping someone locked up for life correcting him, helping him, adding him back as a contributing member of the Herd? It isn't, obviously. That's a different issue, though.)

Also, there was a term once called "Four Walling." It's an old term, back to the days when movie theaters were King. A new movie coming out might have an unusual number of posters set out everywhere. As if on all four walls everywhere you go, there's that poster! Must be a heck of a good movie! And everyone went to see it on opening night, and no one went back, because those "four walled" movies were pretty much always dogs.

Any ad sufficiently annoying, sufficiently over-pushed will cause me to boycott that product – forever. I do not reward such behavior. Neither should you.

I have a personal rule that if a piece of software presents me with ads too many times, I uninstall it. Free or not, I don't want ads. I will not tolerate them. I gave up mainstream television over 30 years ago because there was no freaking way I was going to pay for cable and still have to tolerate commercials, which was how television was "paid for" all along up to that point[39].

---

[39] Oddly, that's now called "free TV" by some. Which it most definitely is not, never was. We were paying for it with the most limited coins we have: the minutes of our lives. It was never free!

Some software starts advertising at me and I drop it. Unfortunately, even some really good software has stated doing this. Adobe products, in their free versions are pretty quiet and tame. But pay for the upgrade and suddenly the system can not leave you alone! Tip and Hint here. Ad for another product there! I just upgraded; give me a gold star! Ahhhhhhhhh!

So, I uninstalled pay-for-it Adobe and went back to the free versions of things. Found other competitive products in some cases. No ads. No non-stop "tips" that I don't need and can't turn off[40].

Microsoft does this with Windows now. The search popup window, for example, every day I am closing the "AI Copilot" ad and the "Edge" ad[41]. And every day those ads come back. I have found (so far) no way to eliminate them permanently. If Microsoft wants to use my computer and my attention as its own channel for heavy advertising and programming (the human sort, not the computer sort) then they can bloody well pay for the computer.

Unfortunately, Microsoft gets away with constantly inserting their flawed and false agenda into the operating system because there's no real way to stop their doing it, and I can't uninstall windows unless I'm willing to finally switch to Linux once and for all[42].

They also get away with it because there's no law providing the consumer with shelter from advertising. Freedom from Advertising, wouldn't that be a nice Constitutional Amendment? (Sign me up!)

---

[40] Which is actually another form of advertising.
[41] Edge is the worst browser on the market, in spite of the advertising claiming otherwise. It's the slowest and least secure, and the most invasive, and most invested in getting into your life, like it or not.
[42] I am definitely getting there, though. I like Linux! It's fast, clean, fast and doesn't need a gold star every time it rolls over. And it's free! Oh, and did I mention it's fast?

Short version: I personally assume the "rule" that anything that pushes itself too hard, advertises itself too much, makes too many fake-smile scenarios around its products, is most likely a bad product and at the least is put out by a predatory company, or at least by a company that sees no problems with predatory ad campaigns put out for them by their advertising agency. Such a company can not to be trusted, can it?

Advertise too much, annoy me too often with products I have no need for (and most people have no need for, especially) and I will drop you like a hot rock.

Over advertising backfires on me.

Question: why doesn't it backfire on the Masses? If only it would, we could all live in a quieter, saner world.

Or maybe it does backfire on the masses, too. How do we know that certain products wouldn't sell better with simple, light weight and absolutely honest advertising?

Now, just sign up here, to support the Quieter World Campaign. Just need your name, email, smart phone number and at least three separate credit cards. No risk… *guaranteed. Really.*

The Too Many Lawyers Rule

90% of all lawyers exist only to protect us from that same 90% of all lawyers.

I came up with that statement a number of years ago. I have since run it by no fewer than 25 lawyers, retired or practicing, and a couple of law students as well. So far, not a single one has even hesitated in agreeing with it. Admittedly, 25 is a small sample group, but not even one disagreement?

Let's say it flat out: we have far too many lawyers in the world. There simply isn't that much for them to do. So they create jobs and niches for themselves. Law suits. Funny contracts. Empty holding companies whose only purpose is to shield against liability and even against paying their bills. (How some billionaires get to be billionaires, by crafting complicated shells with no assets and the claims for bills and payments and live-up-to-your-end-of-the-deal stop there.)

In America alone, 3000 new lawyers are graduated each year. Believe me, they aren't retiring at that same rate.

Twist the law. Circumvent the law. Make a new precedent here. Win a lawsuit there. (Or lose a law suit through gross incompetence – see the George Harrison Lesson on that one.)

Lawyers. Supposed to honor the law. Worship the law. Uphold the hold. Phooey.

LAW-yer.

There was a reason why John Adams[43] wanted, after the Declaration and after they had become their own nation, etc, to make it illegal for lawyers to hold office in Congress. And him a lawyer, go figure, right?

---

[43]The main guy – generally – who made American independence happen. Well, one of several who make it happen. But a very visible figure in that process.

Adams' Laws

The argument was very simple: to be in a position to both craft the law and then to exploit the law was a conflict of interest. And it is. Seems pretty clear right?

Unfortunately, the rest of Congress was also mostly lawyers. So the motion was defeated. And even today folks consider that a law degree is an essential step in getting "inside" in Washington DC.

Unfortunately, conflict of interest is now taken as just an opportunity to exploit, on many levels, by many folks. (Not going further into that one just now.)

Try these on:
- May be hot after heating (might be?)
- Do not turn this package over (printed on the bottom of the package, really!)
- No user serviceable parts inside
- Your mileage may vary (may?)
- Was made in a plant that also processes peanuts
- May contain some bone
- Do not use if you can not clearly read these instructions (eh? What was that, sonny?)
- This product should not be fed to fish (on a bottle of dog shampoo)
- Do not drive with sun shield in place (on a solid, cardboard sun shield)
- This is not a protective device (on a popcorn holder, shaped like a helmet)
- Caution: hot beverages are hot (hard to argue with that one)
- Caution: shoots rubber bands (on a product called "Rubber Band Shooter")
- Not for weight control (on a package of breath mints)
- Caution: do not drive or operate machinery (on a bottle of *children's* cough medicine)
- Wearing this garment does not enable you to fly (on a child's superman outfit)

- Warning: may contain nuts (on a package of nuts!!)
- Remove occupants from stroller before folding it (do I have to?)
- Check the rear seat for children (on almost all modern cars – really? Like I would forget?)
- Not dishwasher safe (on a TV remote control! Remind to get a washable one next time.)

What was all that? Those, and thousands of others, are all of them *real* product label warnings. But, you know what they really are? **They are Lawyer Footprints.** Every one of those represents a lawsuit at some time. Some lawyer actually sued some company for failing to state the incredibly obvious, and almost always won.

Of course they won: juries love to award Big Cash Prizes (except… see the Ford Pinto Lesson).

When a company loses a silly law-suit they put a warning on the package sufficient to keep it from happening again. Until some clever predatory lawyer figures out how to subvert the letter of the warning, rather than the spirit of the warning and sue them again. At which time the warning will be added to or amended. If the company is still in business after that.

Well… it's harmless, you say. Really? *Why would you say that?*

It is not harmless. Those warnings cost money. A few years back, the FDA required all food products to have new labels on them. The manufacturers *all* objected saying it would cost far, far too much to change the labels. (Huh?) Well, on that argument, changing a label is a cost added to the price of the product. OK, how much can that be? Not much, but…

(OK, I'm perhaps silly here in pointing out that the food manufacturers greatly resisted the new labeling requirements, with an extremely flimsy argument. If you watch carefully, you'll see a lot of flimsy arguments being used all over the place. Watch for those; they are indicators of something going on…

but what might not be exactly clear [said *Buffalo Springfield*, once upon a when].)

The real cost is the money lost in the law suit and now that company has to keep at least that much more money in reserve at all times against possible future law suits. Well, that comes out of their profits, right? WRONG! It gets added to the price tag of the product. Be certain that nothing comes out of their profits. Ever.

All costs ultimately go back to the Great Consumer. He pays through the nose for all this stuff. Some one person wins a 10-million-dollar law suit, and everyone else pays the 10 million back to the company. (And the raised price never comes back down, even after the 10 million has been recovered. So really, the company wins, in the long run. If they survived the suit, that is.)

Another issue with too many lawyers, aside from the commercial, I heard a senator once say that we don't know what a piece of legislation really is going to do until it's brought in to court for the first time. Then we get to see what it actually does or what becomes of it. Huh? If the wording of the bill wasn't clear, why was it passed? If it was clear, how can we be at all unsure of what a court will do with it? Well, in case you haven't figured it out yet, it's not the *court* that's unpredictable, but the lawyers themselves.

And if that's true, why do so many believe that those in Congress should be lawyers? If it's still up to the courts to figure out what the bill means?[44]

Here's the short version: too many lawyers means far too many of them are simply parasites[45], no longer upholding the

---

[44]There's actually a fairly simple solution to this, by the way, but it's outside the scope of this present article. See my legal staff for clarification, and be sure your mileage has already varied.

[45]Parasite, as in making a living by eating other people's resources rather than generating one's own resources. This is NOT meant to say that's all the lawyers are. Certainly not. There are many fine people working the legal professions, who are quite aware of this problem. And

law, preserving the rights of all under the law, but now actively exploiting holes in the law, crafting more loopholes, and turning it all in an extremely profitable circus where no one actually wins. No one at all.

Not even the parasite, ultimately.

Too many lawyers. They've contributed greatly the general insanity and chaos of the so-called Modern World.

Remember: 90% of all lawyers exist only to protect us from that same 90% of all lawyers.

---

remember how I started this article? With the fact that many lawyers agree with my evaluation.

The World's Best Clam Chowder Lesson

The Oregon Coast is host to a strange phenomenon. All up and down the coast you'll see signs from various small restaurants and "chowder houses" proclaiming they have the "world's best clam chowder." (Perhaps the East Coast as well?)

Really? Do they all have the best chowder? All of them?

Only if they all get it out of the same can.

A friend of mine, a restaurateur, once proclaimed in front of his establish that he had the world's *worst* clam chowder. He made his own, there in the kitchen, and he solemnly told me that the secret ingredient was clams. (As in, a lot of clams, don't just wave a clam over the mixture while cooking it and call it good.)

His ad campaign was quite effective. (Until the 2007 / 2008 economic meltdown, which did a lot of damage that the banks – who caused that meltdown, yet were never made fully responsible for.)

This one is short: the better a product claims to be, especially without substantiation, the more suspicious you should be. The Hitler / Goebbels law about the Bigger the Lie the more folks will fall for it, simply indicates that the bulk of people never question what they hear or see.

The People let these unlikely and silly statements slip on by, sometimes with quiet misgivings never voiced, sometimes with joyous naivete; either way it's the People who support this heinous practice, if nothing else by simply allowing it.

A proclamation of superior quality, especially the totally absurd and grandiose claim of "world's best" should always be taken as "false until proven true" and mostly such a claim is absolutely impossible to prove.

Unfortunately, that's just the way it is.

The Wrong Side of the Fence Rule

I was highly disappointed when I first heard the term "co-dependent." Or rather, when I first understood what it meant. On first hearing the term, I was very excited! Wow, I thought, somebody's finally defined what a proper, functional relationship is: cooperative interdependence. Boy... was I wrong.

Co-dependency is simply another label and pseudo-explanation for the bad ways in which people get along, or fail to get along, reinforcing each other's rotten behavior in the process.

Dang it.

So I began to wonder, why has psychology / social psychology never defined Healthy, in their terms.[46]

Psychology seems to love to define conditions, neuroses, psychoses and all the other "-oses" and no matter how much or how little progress they make in treating such conditions (usually very little) they continue to delight in creating more labels.

Alas for them, giving a thing a label does *not* treat it, or cure it. Or really actually explain it.

So, if we in actuality have no definition for what "sane" is, why would that be?

My theory is two-fold. First, many of the practitioners of these very difficult fields (psychology is not to be underestimated in its complexity) would never think of it. The

---

[46]Come to think of it, not sure AMA Medicine has ever actually defined healthy either. They can define all the ways in which you might not be healthy, leaving Healthy, then, as an absence of absence of known illness. Not good enough.

idea that healthy / sane has never been defined might even surprise them.

The second part is this: those few who might notice that a healthy relationship has no role model, and a fully functional human mind has no role model and no definition, have no desire to go there, against the possibility of finding themselves on the wrong side of that newly crafted dividing line, a dividing line that, being on the wrong side of which, means you're not really playing with a full deck.

What psychologist would want find himself in that situation? Of having to admit he's not "perfectly healthy?"

But in our society, who is? Or, rather, without a proper definition, how could we possibly tell who's healthy / sane and who's not?

The Brick Layer Rule

Actually, this one's pretty simple and pretty profound, all the same. It speaks to Human behavior in profound ways, really, most of which I won't really go into. They'll be obvious, either immediately or gradually over time as this rule sinks in.

Here it is, in a nutshell. Take any simple task, such a laying bricks. (Not saying laying bricks is really, really simple, this is just for argument's sake. But it is simple, so there.) A person can put down bricks and build up walls, fireplaces, walkways and many things make of bricks. Over the years, his technique gets better, more creative, more sophisticated. By the end of his career he has made so many improvements and innovations to the original art as he was taught it that – guess what? It will now take those following him a lifetime to master those techniques[47].

Humans are like that. Ants have been content to do what they do without much change (that we know of) for millions of years (that we know of). Humans? Always innovating. Ants have been taught by Nature (or Their Nature, or by Gaia, or by God, as you may wish) how to do what they do. Humans? They had to invent all the arts that ants simply do. Maybe because ants are simply "programmed that way." Maybe.

Humans, on the other hand, having to invent everything they do, are then left with the possibility of continuing to create it, continuing to make it up, to make it better, to be innovative.

Spend a life time mastering a thing and you have created something that now requires a life time to master. (More or less, variations in creativity, intelligence and willingness to learn… well, your mileage may vary, if it hasn't already[48].)

---

[47]Well, maybe not a life time. The first guy blazed the trail and those that follow can learn his technique quickly, perhaps. But you get my point? Yes? No?

[48]Yeppers… your mileage has already varied. Really.

The "Grasshopper" Rule

This is a good one to follow the Brick Layer Rule, for it's also about mastery, and mastery in and of the Human condition.

People take on crafts, jobs, things to do, and in the course of their lives they might or might not rise to the level of Mastery of the craft. True masters are rare, unfortunately, for it often takes serious dedication and discipline, plus enthusiasm and creativity to get there. Some few folks are lucky enough to be born masters of anything they put their wits to. Yay them! But for the rest of us, it usually means long and dedicated work to achieve mastery.

There's a rule of thumb in the computer industry – or used to be; it's sort of ignored now. After college, it takes about 18 years more or less, of 60 hours a week to make a master programmer. It's a complex art. Unfortunately, the industry has dumbed-down the art, accepting far lower quality and is enjoying far less innovation as a consequence.

(But hey, it costs less, so it must be good right? Dang employees, anyway, right? Right?)

You can spot a master. It's actually pretty easy. A master of any art makes his work seem so very, very simple. And he's usually very calm and self-certain about it, too. That's how you can spot a master. No anxiety, no worries, no *effort*. Seemingly, at least.

The young student standing in front of the master is amazed that the blind master can "hear" the grasshopper at his feet. On asking, "Master, how is it that you can hear the grasshopper?" The master replies, quite rightly (though also a little irritatingly), "how is it that you do not?"

Later on (in this old TV show[49]) as the young man has grown up under his master's tutelage – now known by the name "Grasshopper"[50] of course – he, too, can hear the grasshopper.

Masters: they make it look simple.

Beware, however: some will substitute bluster, force, anger, snake-oil arguments and double-talk in the place of real mastery. Telephone tech-support scam operators will shout nonsensical streams of "techno-babble" strung together in nonsensical ways to get you to buy $100s of dollars worth of software no one needs (or maybe 1 in a 1000 at most needs). Because you can't recognize the babble as babble, they often get their money.

That's not mastery, that's razzle-dazzle[51].

Can you hear the grasshopper yet? (Surprisingly, grasshoppers really do make sounds. It's not that big a trick. It's just paying attention, which sometimes is quite a trick.)

---

[49]*Kung Fu*, with David Carradine, 1972 – 1974.
[50]Yes, that's where that came from.
[51]Though perhaps there is a mastery achievable in the arts of Flim-Flammery.

The Ad Blocker Lesson

Oblivious is as oblivious does…
…to paraphrase the Forest Gump lesson.

I use an ad blocker on my browser (all my browsers). I personally find ads extremely offensive, ever since I was 7 years old and discovered on my own that commercials can lie. All the adults around me were amused by my reaction to this discovery and I was shocked by their lack of one. They just blithely accepted that ads lie and yes, so what? Move along sonny.

Huh?

So, I use an ad blocker. These ads are coming in to my computer, using *my* Internet connection and *my* data bandwidth (which might be on a monthly limitation, fer Pete's sake!) and using *my* computer to assaulting *my* eyes and ears. Surely I have the right to not have them come into my home, yes?

Yes. In my world, there would be a Freedom from Advertising Law. What a relief that would be.

Oh well… so I use an ad blocker.

Here's the catch. A great many websites then put up a popup saying, "please turn off your ad blocker. Ads are how we make any money here. So support us by turning it off."

Huh? (Again...)

Did I stutter? You are using *my* computer and *my* Internet bandwidth to show me ads I've already told you (by having an ad blocker) that I don't want. Turning it off is NOT going to support you. Can't you see that if I use an ad blocker then I am extremely unlikely to ever click on an ad? You don't make money by showing an ad, you make money by my clicking on an ad and then actually buying something there.

Do not ask me to turn my ad blocker off. I will simply go to another website. I will *not* support your use of my resources (including my attention) to show me ads I don't want in the first place.

Get over yourself. The purpose of the Internet was never to make *you* money.

In point of fact, I personally have never made a dollar on the Internet. I've put together dozens of websites for various purposes, and not one of them has ever generated a buck. That's really not the purpose of the Internet, though it does work that way for many of you. Good. Excellent even. Just, please, don't force me to participate, when it's frankly quite obvious that I'm never going to click on an ad.

What's the lesson here: I said it at the top: oblivious is as oblivious does. It's also rude.

Don't ask me to turn off my ad blocker. You make money by providing a service, not by assaulting me with ads.

The Skyrim Rule

Bethesda Softworks is a profoundly good software manufacturer[52]. They make some very fine games, often with great and subtle embedded messages of a fine moral or educative nature. They've been very successful.

(Unfortunately, they are now owned by Microsoft, so in the future this preeminence and quality may suffer. Time will tell us. Beside the point, though...)

One of their games, Skyrim, is a fantasy action-adventure game, involving exploration, running freely around in a wondrous and magical world, working toward saving that world from a serious problem.

Alright, good, solid, mythic adventure.

Oops... out of the box it wouldn't play. That is, it would play, but it was impossible to finish the main story line, the main quest, as it's called.

Huh?

To my knowledge they never did fix that themselves. That and literally 1000s of other bugs were fixed, enthusiastically even, but the community of fans and players. The "unofficial patch" became absolutely essential to play the game.

Only you had to explore around on the Internet, ask other players and so forth to find out that there even was such a patch available.

The kicker? Regardless of this, Skyrim was voted Game of the Year! (2011, naturally followed up with by the Game of the Year Edition, a repackaging of the product that still didn't fix the main quest! Sheesh.)

Huh?

---

[52]Although they've also made some serious dogs and some very serious guffaws on their main stream products. Oh well... guess that means they're Human like the rest of us. Read on.

You couldn't finish the main quest? Lots of little quests were totally broken? You could get stuck in certain places and lost in certain others and... and... and that's game of the year?

1000s of the bugs fixed by the *consumers*? Game of the Year?

Wow. Just think about that one. The ramifications are legion, in all sorts of directions.

(And they've done better since then. Thank'ee Sai.)

The *Day After Tomorrow* Lesson

The Day After Tomorrow was a movie made in 2004. It was an "end of the world" movie centered around one possibility for climate change. A real possibility, by the way.

At the time, NPR interviewed three world-class meteorologists about the movie, and they concluded rather emphatically that it was good, well done, accurate, save only on the time scale. In the movie this all took place within days. In reality, should those events occur, the effects would take longer to happen.

One of them said, "yep, about right."

The second one said, "yep, about right."

The third one said, "it'll be worse than that."

That was 2004 when climate change was barely a household term[53].

So, in the wake of such a movie, why are we *still* debating climate change? Because it was "just a movie."

Once something is turned into a movie, too many people can then simply dismiss it as fiction. Even movies based on facts are often considered fiction[54].

The Day After Tomorrow made perfectly clear one possibility of what we may be facing in the all too near future. Yet it's now a nearly forgotten movie. (Made worse, in fact, because that same director went on to destroy the world two more times: in *2012* and in the *Independence Day* movies. So obviously it's all just fiction, right?)

---

[53]Though many and many had been shouting it from the rooftops for 50 years and more already by that point. It's been a long hard climb to get global warming / climate change recognized as real possibility.

[54]On the other hand, too many people take fiction movies and treat them as real. Go figure...

The lesson is nothing more than this: even a truth, cast as a movie will mostly like then be pigeon-holed as fiction. Actually, a spectacular action movie is a good way to bury a truth, right out in the open, where no one will see it.

The George Harrison Lesson

George Harrison, one of the Beatles, some years after the Beatles, had a hit single: *My Sweet Lord*. He was sued for plagiarism over this, though the so-called original song had barely any similarity to his new hit. (I won't go in to details here; you can look it up.)

Here's the weird part: the judge concluded that it was *unconscious* plagiarism and so found against Mr Harrison.

Huh? *Excuse me?*

I don't know whether to hate the judge or George's lawyer more.

Either way, surely that judgment was nuts.

But also surely that judgment could have been appealed on the basis that the judge was prejudiced (at best) or, more likely, utterly unqualified to hear cases concerning the music industry.

Listen to Beethoven's 9th Symphony, you'll find several measures that that overlap with *A Little Help from My Friends*. This goes on all the time in music, writing and all the arts. It's said that all writers steal material from each other. Do they object? Not really. It's normal. If you know any music at all, you'll hear how very, very often pieces overlap, borrow from each other, and even accidentally sound like pieces of each other. How could it be otherwise?

What if every news channel had to post only new and wholly original articles? (That might be refreshing, actually.) Instead, we have the same stories showing up on 100s of separate "news" outlets. Sometimes it seems that the TV channels simply get their news from the Internet, for I hear stories (on those rare cases where I happen to be near a TV) being reported as brand new but are things I read on the Internet 24 to 48 hours earlier.

Unconscious and even conscious plagiarism is normal and expected in many creative arts, such as writing, painting and music. As for journalism... well, let's not go there right now.

That judge should have been fired. (Or the case appealed, at the least.)

Poor George. He never did have any luck.

What's the lesson? Think on it. There are actually several I could spin from this point, but the significant part has been stated.

(These stories are themselves the important part, as with all "teaching tales" it's the story more than the conclusion that matters. Make of the story what you will, since that's all we each can do anyway, right?)

The Xenomorph Lesson

In the movie *Aliens*, the 2nd movie in the series, they made an interesting statement at one point, early-ish in the movie.

Our heroine, played by Sigourney Weaver, is on her way back to that awful planet, where the creature was picked up that ate her entire crew.

This time she's backed by a squad of space marines. The mission is being explained to the marines and the statement is made that "a xenomorph may be involved."

Apparently, few people in the land of Aliens Fandom understood what that word actually means. They have taken it to be the name of the face-hugging, chest-bursting species.

Wrong!

It's a simple bit of Latin meaning "foreign shape"... that is, non-humanoid[55]. Not shaped like people. At least, not like people as we know them.

Xenomorph.

Look it up on the Internet, look up xenomorph and you'll get pictures from the movies, specifically of the face-huggers. *Wrong!* (Seriously, just wrong!)

That I know of, that species was never actually named.

So, there was a reason why we used to teach Greek and Latin in schools. It's not a luxury, it's not intellectual snobbishness either. These are the roots for many words used in

---

[55] And even worse, one of the Star Trek movies even misused the word Humanoid, as in some Klingons calling the United Federation of Planets was a "humanoids only" club, meaning, in that case, it was not Klingons. But Klingons are HUMANOID! It means human shaped. Hello?

our culture even now, 60 years after the Roman Catholic Church gave up masses in Latin[56], it still matters!

Xeno and morph: "foreign" and "shape." Very simple... But apparently not really.

OK, the lesson? People will walk straight by a word they don't understand, especially when they think they *do* understand it. They'll wander right on by with a misunderstanding and never even notice.

"Xenomorph" is a light-weight example, maybe, but the principal is quite real and potentially very serious.

Dang.

---

[56]Though I have heard some folks say even now that Latin is "the only language God understands" and that the decision to do away with Latin masses was of the Devil. Let's just say, I lack data on that...

The Microsoft Lesson or, Why Corporations Fail

There's a problem with the current, standard model under which "major" corporations operate these days. Yet none of them seem to have noticed, even after Lee Iaccoca wrote books and left a magnificent example of how to run thing better. And if the corporate world can ignore *him* then what chance to do any of *us* have for changing things?

(No need, in time the Mega Corporations will simply die out, it's inevitable, the way things are going. Which is part of the point of this particular article.)

There are many specific examples, but I seem to be hooked on putting Microsoft specifically over the coals. But this applies equally to others such as Apple Corporation, GM and Starbucks, among a great many others.

Microsoft was started by an entrepreneur and a visionary. Bill Gates had a personal mission, to bring technology to the world. (He, along with many others, working together, surely did forge the world we live in now.)

Under his leadership, his choices, and always under his vision, Microsoft grew to be bigger than IBM, about the time that (early 90s) IBM laid off in one swell foop (as they say) more employees than Microsoft even had. This was back when Bill was known (affectionately) inside the company as the "Six Billion Dollar Bill[57]."

Then the political games started, in-fighting, power grabs and struggles. Bill kept control but – apparently (*apparently*

---

[57] I met many Microsoft employees during that era, and they expressed a seeming genuine loyalty and admiration for Bill. I believe it was genuine. I met him myself a couple of times, and he was quite available, "just another guy" as the expression goes. You could talk to him, unlike *every* other major CEO I have ever met.

only, mind) – he eventually got tired of those games and relinquished control of the company, retiring to an advisory capacity and eventually walking away entirely[58].

At that point (2005 ± some) Microsoft began it's slow spiral downward[59]. Windows Vista was the first version of Windows to come out not on Bill's watch. It was a very bad operating system[60].

This was followed by Windows 8, a creature so bad that Microsoft's next version was 10, not 9. As if MSFT was trying to distance themselves from 8, and that's as close to an apology as they ever came, though in their strange way that's exactly what it was.

Windows 10 was OK, not great, but OK. It was not as bad as the previous versions, Vista and 8, but it was no where near as good, as fast or as reliable as XP had been[61].

Now there's Windows 11 and the reception to 11 had been very cool industry wide. It's not actually worse than 10, neither is it any better. In fact, there's nothing to warrant giving it a new number at all. Just a style change. Alteration of colors and a complete rearrangement of where things are. Pointless update, in other words[62].

Oh well… That's the brief history.

---

[58] I would say "walking away in disgust" only I have no such data; it's just a hunch.
[59] Slow at the start, faster now. Like a plane out of control. "Roll vertical and auger in" is the unhumorous expression.
[60] Some of the subtleties of why Vista was such a bad Operating System might be lost unless you also are a programmer and/or an aficionado of operating systems. Take my word for it – or don't, your choice
[61] XP was the last version of Windows produced entirely on Bill Gates' watch, by the way.
[62] It's possible I've missed on important quality of 11, but research and even perusing the "Why 11 is Great" postings (infomercials backed by MSFT? Hard to tell, the Internet these days being what it is) I can find nothing that warrants a new number. Is it possible they went to 11 *only* because Apple did? That would be incredibly petty, even for M$FT.

Combine that with their newest tactic of buying up the 2nd and 3rd largest game companies on the planet, giving them, along with their own X-BOX brand, the top three game brands. Plus, they've acquired other things lately, and farmed out some of their standard and long-standing software to outside companies to maintain, improve or destroy as they will. In short, Microsoft is doing less and less programming, certainly less that's worth anything much, and is buying up successful enterprises, farming what should be in-house work to 3rd party contractors, relegated all their technical support to firms in India, who – in my experience (and in that only) – are not as qualified as was Microsoft's own tech support staff back when Bill was running things[63].

[Tech support all over the world now very often a frustrating experience. The industry as a whole has forgotten what tech support is: the only direct contact their customers will ever have with the company, making it critical to do the very best you possibly can for your customers.]

Put all that together and it's safe to say that Microsoft is gradually getting out of the software business, becoming a holding company and a distribution point for the software tinkered together by others. And – very important point here – they don't fix their bugs[64]!

All that is fact (more or less, to the best of my knowledge, your mileage has already varied, and all that), taking all that into account, Microsoft is clearly on the way out. Or at least on the way out as any sort of leader in the computer industry, unless one can be a leader without actually *doing* anything

---

[63] I had reason to be on the phone with them more than once, for advanced problems and programming / development issues. They were courteous, friendly and quite knowledgeable… unlike too much of tech support these days.

[64] There are bugs in Windows and Office that've been there for 20+ years, and still no sign of ever being fixed. Which is part of why Linux and LibreOffice are doing so well now. *Those* are being actively developed and supported.

significant in computers or software. Or to put it in better business lingo, they are gradually transforming into something else, perhaps a holding company, or maybe an investment firm in some subtle and slight-of-hand fashion.

In the meantime, their market share for Windows has dropped from 95%+ to about 75% now. Windows 11 especially created a great *hooraw* among developers, power uses and gamers[65], and there are more and more postings on the Internet of the "I've absolutely *had it* with Windows, how do I get into Linux quickly?" and such.

The thing is, Linux is a vastly superior product, actively being worked on, optimized for best performance, configurable, user-friend in a way Windows long since has given up trying to be. It's also available in many "flavors" (their term, not mine) depending on your needs and likes.

It's very fast, far more reliable than Windows, and all that.

Big deal, right? That isn't the point of this article. Just the background.

Microsoft, compared to what it was under Bill's control, has failed and is failing. They (the management and stock holders) seem either to have not noticed or to not care. My guess is that as a corporation they don't respect software anymore (confirmed by at least one inside source at M$FT), and are in process of transforming themselves in to something else. Just a big corporation that actually no longer has a true purpose, just money.

A purposeless operation is just that: something without reason to exist. In the long run it will fail, but it may become a problem in the meantime.

What's the short version of this story? What was a great and highly productive company, under the guidance of

---

[65]Gamers are a large and important segment of computer users, believe me or not. Computer games have always demanded the very highest performance of both the hardware and the operating system. It's even a big part of what continues to drive computer development.

creativity and vision, has become just another boring drag-weight on the fabric of our times. They "make money" now by putting over a great and huge fraud. They seem no longer capable of creating a truly improved version of Windows or of Office. Though, evidently, their games division is doing quite well.

I am *not* saying that Microsoft is a problem and should be disbanded. This is just an example, and just a story. My story. That's all.

And they all lived happily ever after.
Good night.

The White Album Rule

Many years ago, the Beatles, the archetypal rock-and-roll band – who permanently changed our world by simply singing to us – put out an album.[66] A very successful one[67].

The Beatles did a lot of experimental and ground-breaking stuff with their art and craft. One of those became a classic, the White Album, so called because it was in a plain white cover. But... it was also numbered. Each album was therefore unique, and a collectors' thing. It was an instant smash hit. Sold out.

Then came along CDs. Guess what? The white album was re-released, in a numbered edition as a CD. White cover. Numbered. And guess what? People bought the white album again. (Some for the first time, of course, but many who already had it on vinyl bought it again on CD anyway. Go figure.)

In the movie *Men in Black* the character played by Tommy Lee Jones is giving the character played by Will Smith a tour of "alien technology" they have acquired. One of those things is a super tiny disk thing that he says will replace CDs soon. "We'll all have to buy the white album again," he says.

Cool.

And that makes my point.

---

[66]Back in the Olden Days musicians used to put out complete collections of recordings, often related to each other in some fashion. When recorded as a series of wavy bumps on a vinyl surface, it was called an album – and many say it was superior sound to the new(er) digital pattern encoded optically on super smooth surface covered in plastic, or to the digital stream you might grab off the Internet with some music service who keeps your collection for you, but still charges you money to listen to it. (How's that working out for you, by the way? We *owned* collections of music, and could listen to them anytime, without having to pay the butler for fetching it for us.)

[67]Actually, they were all successful. That's one of the qualities of the Beetles. They were professionals and perfectionists.

Even a numbered collectors' item can be sold again and again. Each one unique, but actually so many of them that the uniqueness is lost and becomes merely a marketing ploy. However, an unopened, original White Album on vinyl currently sells for anything from $3,000 to $8,000, depending on the serial number. A lower serial number is more valuable than a higher number.

Collectors. They'll buy anything.

Again, and again, and again…

The *Last of the Samurai* Lesson

In some ways the Tom Cruise movie *The Last Samurai* was a triumph, beautifully executed, gorgeously photographed, rich and epic in scope. In one way, however, it was absolutely horrifying. (Horrifying, not horrible.)

It was horrifying in that it pretty accurately depicted the end of the samurai. Pretty accurately: there was no one battle where this dedicated breed of servants[68] was finally removed, so the events are what Hollywood likes to call "compressed," but baring that, it's does justice to history.

Tom Cruise's character is fictional, but again not at odds against history, not really.

Why was this horrifying? Here was an entire people, a village of people, dedicated to the service of the Emperor in the way of Bushido, in the way of the Samurai. Every day they'd get up and practice their arts, continue to perfect every action of their day, every action of their lives. A level of dedication rarely seen in the world any more. Magnificent professionals.

But... what happened? Those eager to embrace Western Culture and especially Western *wealth* saw the Samurai as a hindrance, for the Samurai themselves saw Western Culture as a threat to the emperor. Accurately, did they see. But greed won out, so an effort to wipe out the Samurai was put into action.

How do normal soldiers stand against a single Samurai, let alone an army of such?

Easy. Canons, and Gatling Guns. In a few weeks a soldier who can turn a crank can himself be cranked out and the

---

[68]Servants, yes. The word "samurai" means servant. Let that one soak in for a bit.

magnificent, dedicated, finely trained, finely honed Samurai is simply mowed down. Poof.

Automation in the hands of a barely trained near nobody, does away with a life-time of dedication and centuries long tradition of service.

And now those skills are mostly lost. Even the desire for that sort of mastery is largely lost. We play video games and watch movies that give us a taste of such things – *Super Powers*, as it were – and that seems to be enough for us now.

When automation replaces skill, you've lost something that might never be recovered. Great skill was rare and cherished. But an army of people who can turn the crank on a gatling gun replaces both superlative skill and the wisdom to know when to draw your sword, or turn that crank.

What wisdom did that soldier gain in his few weeks of training, versus the Samurai dedicated to a lifetime of professionalism and service? Wisdom cannot be implanted; only the individual himself can acquire that wisdom, mostly through paying close attention all the time and constantly striving "to be better."

The Plain Hot Dog Lesson

This one's pretty simple. Maybe even one of my very first "rules" gleaned from observation and experience.

I used to study martial arts. Long and long ago (not in the time of the Samurai, unfortunately, but long enough ago). After a lesson or a workout at the dojo, I'd often get a hot dog and drink from the hot dog stand[69] that happened to be off the same parking lot. The proprietor never got used to my ordering all my hot dogs plain. No mustard, No relish. No sauerkraut. No ketchup[70]. No nothing on it. Plain hot dog, on plain bun.

They were good hot dogs. They didn't need anything.

But the proprietor's reaction got me to thinking about it. Why is it so incredibly normal to put all that stuff on to a hot dog? Why was he so surprised that I wanted it plain?

Partly because it's just so very normal, an 'everyone does it' kind of thing. But mostly, I suspect, because most hot dogs aren't worth eating on their own. Yuck, in fact.

Here's the rule, then: if it's not good enough to eat plain, it's not good enough to eat. Period.

All those extras are there to hide the fact that 1, a hot dog is considerably smaller than they used to be (long and long ago) and 2, they actually taste pretty awful, all by themselves. But with all that *stuff* on one you won't really notice either problem!

Phooey... you put out an inferior product because most people won't notice. You'll lose a few customers, but the savings in profit margin more than makes up for it and you come out ahead.

---

[69]This was before I learned how bad such mainstream food is for you. I was young, what can I say?

[70]Nor "catsup" – which was simply a dodge to get around a law put into place attempting to corner a monopoly on this largely disgusting sauce [disgusting once you know what it's really made from – ahhh!]

Geez, Louise! (as they say).

Worse, as a new generation comes along, they accept the "new-and-improved" hot dog as a normal one, never knowing that it's now actually inferior. No, this is normal! So the process continues. Once it's normal, you can then sneak the quality down even more and keep increasing your profits. Eventually it's not even food any more, but who cares? We're *used to it*.

Just hand me some more ketchup / catsup, because this utterly unidentifiable thing I'm eating tastes horrid (or worse, maybe has no taste at all).

Let's all relish this article, but remember not to garnish it up too much. The plain lesson is the point.

The *Banacek* Lesson

This might also be called the Tom Cruise lesson, but Mr Cruise is a real guy and Banacek was a fictional character, and seems safer to use as a role model. Also, fewer people have any preconceptions about Banacek so can take in this lesson more readily. (So there.)

Banacek was fictional person in a series by the same name, which aired around 1972 and lasted for 1 ½ seasons. Would have gone on longer, but George Peppard had to back out, due to some personal issues. Dang it. It was a wonderful series. Though a bit dated now. Our culture isn't liberal enough anymore to embrace the show they way it was done back then. To bring it back it would need some updating.

(So what? *Bring it back!*)

Oh well… and anyway. The character, Thomas Banacek, who went by his last name only, was a supremely confident fellow. Very intelligent, very educated, good taste, fast wits, fast hands when necessary, though he'd walk away from a fight whenever possible. The show was only mildly violent, dealing mostly with locked-room thefts. Impossible thefts, as it were. Very good stuff. Serious brain teasers, and very, very few flaws in any of the logic. Tight stories.

But Banacek himself often rubbed people the wrong way (in the stories). Mostly because of his supreme confidence, backed up by his successes. His confidence and continuous good nature just annoyed some folks.

And that's about all there is to this lesson. Confidence and competence makes some people unhappy.

You could say he could have behaved a little more reservedly, so as not to make people around him unhappy. And I could say, why? He never deliberately offended anyone, unless the other person first chose that mode for their relationship. He was never rude or belittling. He was highly respectful of everybody, at least initially, and would never take advantage of anyone who didn't know what was going on already. That is, he *never* took advantage of anyone.

Incredibly honest and ethical both. He would never took a bribe, though they were offered; he would never even enter into a conflict of interest.

Why should a person like that have to change his behavior, just to keep a few folks from bouncing off of their own poor self-images?

Short version: extreme confidence combined with proven ability simply offends some people. And it's usually their own lack of confidence that is actually being irritated.

The MSG Rule

I hesitate (almost) to bring this one up. Oh well... there it is. Already brought up; can't back out now.

The subject is MSG. Monosodium glutamate, MSG, is a "flavor enhancer[71]" and is used that way.

America's FDA continues to list it as a safe substance. Then why does it kill a few hundred people every year? Chinese Restaurant Syndrome is what it used to called, but today most Chinese restaurants won't use the stuff, and far too many processed / packaged foods do.

It's officially safe, and is therefore legal. Further, manufacturers are allowed to *hide* the fact that they have it in their products, through such euphemisms as natural flavors, artificial flavors, hydrolyzed vegetable protein, spices, and a dozen other names.

Why are they allowed to hide it? Because there was Great Outcry from the public against it, yet officially it's safe. Also because (probably) the manufacturers have become reliant on it to make up for the fact that their products have no flavor otherwise (see also *the Plain Hot Dog Rule*).

When I see a product that says "artificial flavors" or "spices" or any of those catch phrases in their ingredients list, I put it back. Unless the label specifically mentions "no MSG" and even then, I'm cautious, because what that statement is really saying is, "no MSG *that we know of*."

---

[71] Actually, it's not a flavor enhancer at all. What it really does is far more subtle and insidious. It actually produces a compulsion into the person, a compulsion to eat more. You "think" it tastes wonderful, but that's a body-level reaction created by this chemical. It was the first of what is now an entire family of such additives. Phooey...

A popular food product a few years back was advertised as MSG-free, but the owner found out that one of his suppliers was lying about the contents of the spice packet. MSG.

Fact is, MSG is neuroactive substance, affecting neurological function and a bunch of other things in the body. It occurs in nature but in that form, it isn't dangerous, because it occurs along with other substances at the same time – *the whole food*. Used by itself and as an additive to things, you are taking it out of context, as it were, which makes it potentially risky.

Oh, but the AMA says it is OK. Nevertheless, there are plenty of studies [72] demonstrating its hazards, plus much so-called anecdotal evidence. Add to that the fact that it is illegal in some nations, some nations where – apparently – the citizenry matters more than do corporate profits [73].

Short version: just because the government says a thing is safe, doesn't make it so. What's safe for one person, might not be for another. *You* have to be responsible for your own health and food tolerances. You cannot just go with the Herd's idea of normal. "Normal don't exist."

---

[72] You can find the studies online if you dig… but you do have to dig now. The studies used to be easier to find. (Suggestive, yes?) The NIH (!) has published studies showing toxicity of MSG. Many others do too.

[73] What happened to "of the people, by the people, for the people?" If the People don't want it, and make a huge outcry against it, and even other nations have outlawed it, then how can you possibly not do as the People have demanded? Isn't this a representational government? Isn't it?

The Celebrity Rule

(Formerly known as the "O J Simpson Lesson")

Celebrities in our culture are often treated extremely harshly, often found guilty in the "court of public opinion" even over trivial matters, no matter what the facts might later reveal.

People will point fingers at celebrities and denounce them for doing the very things they themselves often do, crying that they should be held to a higher standard.

Why? (I mean really, why?)

Look at the JFK assassination. Right in plain view an American president was shot (twice, by the way), yet the actual assailant is unknown to this day. Or maybe he / they are known. Certainly, the official investigation (the Warren Commission) was a white wash and cover up. But what were they covering up?

Another example might be the OJ Simpson trial. Did OJ actually kill anyone? All I know is that *I* don't know. It also seems that most people (especially at the time) "knew" that he did do it, even though the jury found him innocent[74].

For me, my only source of data being the news, I have no actual data about it and consequently no opinion. (News, especially in a sensational – aka celebrity – case is unreliable. Did he do it? Beats me! Give me the complete *facts* and I'll rummage through them and see what I can come up with. Baring that, forget it.

---

[74]OK, so later on he was tried again civil court and lost most of his money in judgments against him. Even though he was found innocent previously. Ah, but then later again, he was found guilty for armed robbery and given 33 years in prison without parole. Was he doing an armed robbery because he'd lost all his money earlier and couldn't get honest work because he was guilty in the courts of public opinion? Whose fault was it then, really? Just a thought… maybe, myabe not.

To further harp on the JFK example. 1000s of people have "investigated" that event, spun theories, created 3D models of the event, analyzed it in tremendous detail... yet we're left with the "fact" that still no one knows what happened. What do we know? The president was killed on 23 Nov 1963, while on a tour in Texas. Autopsy evidence suggested he was shot twice, but the official report from the Warren Commission concluded a lone gunman and a single "magic bullet" shot. A single bullet that caused no fewer than 3 separate wounds (four?), including one in another passenger in a car. Well, that was obviously not true; bullets don't do that. Why was the official report so blatantly falsified? We can ask those questions, but we have no *data* about what really happened.

The thing is, just because a thing has no data does not keep most (*nearly* all) people from jumping to conclusions anyway. The Human brain is a pattern matching device, with some creativity tossed in. In the absence of a defined pattern it will make one up anyway.

The flip side is that too much attention and too many investigators can just as easily make a mishmash and hodgepodge of what facts are known. Even something seen in plain view by many people can become, in the long run, unknown and unknowable.

Hence conspiracy theories. Lacking data, we spin explanations anyway. This is why celebrities can never possibly have a just and fair trial without it being closed to reporters and the public.

The Law of 42

An extremely successful and popular spoof science-fiction adventure romp om the 1970s-'80s was the *Hitchhiker's Guide the Galaxy*[75].

One aspect of this drama was the concept of the Ultimate Question, you know, the Big One, the question of Life, the Universe and Everything.

After a long series of adventures, it turns out the Answer is "42." Huh?

Well, says the largest computer ever made, you never really defined the question. Again, huh?

But it's the Big Question! The Ultimate Question!

Yes, agrees the computer. But what exactly *is* the question?

Oh. So, it turns out, again after much adventuring, that in any given Universe only the Question or the Answer may be known. Never both. To know both would mean that Universe would have to end and be replaced by something even more inexplicable. (Some say this has already happened.)

What? Or maybe, So? Possibly even *So What?*

I use this imaginative invention to remind myself that we do, indeed, live in a strange Universe. Fact is, the deeper you look at things, the more questions you find, instead of answers. Ultimately, there are no answers in this Universe (so we conclude, therefore, that *the Hitchhiker's Guide* takes place in another Universe, since here we have only questions, there they have only the answer, and no answer here equals 42 (save perhaps what's 6 x 7, of course).

---

[75] I do not mean that awful movie version that was made for the American audience. Badly directly, badly written. Horrible. All the life had been stripped from it. I mean the original "radio" presentation and the books, and the first BBC video production, which featured many of the same actors as the radio drama did.

It's true, you know. Around 1890 they had actually concluded that just everything that could be known was known, that only refinements and additional decimal points was all that was left to discover. Engineering, in other words. "Science" was done. Oops. Then came Einstein and Schwartzchild and all the rest of those amazing thinkers, and suddenly almost nothing that we thought we knew turned out to be more than very loosely accurate or only the surface of the matter.

Ever since then the deeper we look (or the farther out we look) the more questions we find. Even when we think we have an answer, it often turns out that the answer is not correct or not complete.

The James Webb telescope is doing it again. Many of the standing theories of the Universe, including even how old it is, are suddenly thrown in to chaos, once again. No Answers. Only Questions.

Isn't that cool? I mean, really? Cooooool.

Epilogue

As *A Funny Thing Happened on the Way to the Forum* said (or sang) at its ending, what is the moral? Must be a moral! Frankly? Beats me.

This is a crazy time for a crazy species, on a crazily overcrowded planet, crazily close to the edge of disaster[76].

OK, I do run into people who legitimately believe we are *not* overpopulated, badly polluted, or super-saturated with other people's agendas. They believe our society is perfectly OK as it is. I hope they are right, and that I am wrong.

I welcome being wrong, as it's a chance to learn something new. (At least I try to welcome it. Sometimes it is annoying, though... dang it.)

I hope some of these personal observations are of use to you. Or at least get you thinking a bit. Maybe you can come with your own Rules. Sarah's Rules, or Jason's Lessons, or Dmitri's Laws. Why not?

Think, dang it! Think for yourself. Think it through.

If you can't explain easily and quickly why you did whatever you just did, then it's time to sit down, and think it through. Why *did* you do that? Find out why you did it, and maybe you'll be horrified by it all. Or maybe you'll realize that it really was the right thing to do, only now you *know* that it was.

Don't let anyone tell you what to think or believe. Not the news. Not even me.

Except I'm always right, of course. (Uh, huh... sure.)

Final note: here's a classic teaching story usually credited to various Taoist teachers.

---

[76] And close to the edge of the galaxy it swims in, but I can't see that that's actually relevant.

A farmer wakes up one morning to find his stallion has broken out during the night.

"Oh what bad luck," say the neighbors.

"Good, bad? Who can say," says the farmer.

Two days later, the stallion returns with three mares accompanying him.

"Oh what good luck!" say the neighbors

"Good? Bad?" says the farmer. "Who can say?"

Sometime after that the farmer's son is breaking the mares, only to get thrown and break a leg.

"Oh what bad luck," say the neighbors.

"Good? Bad? Who can say?"

A short time later a warlord comes through the village, recruiting by force all able-bodied men. Of course, the farmer's son cannot be taken.

Good? Bad? Who can say?

~ Jeff

Biographical Note

Jeffrey P Adams, XyZ, is a self-employed entrepreneur and raconteur. He lives in various places, mainly North America and is for the most part self-educated, but with some academic experience. Fortunately, not too much of the latter.

He writes under various pseudonyms (oh-oh, shouldn't have mentioned that – never mind, didn't say that) and admires Great Writers, most Cats, Folks of Integrity and especially Thunderstorms. He is a fan of rational behavior, of thinking things through, and of being personally responsible for everything. He remembers the *21st Century* TV program, hosted by Walter Cronkite, and is sure this isn't *that* 21st Century. We must have skipped to a parallel Universe somewhere along the way.

By the way, if asked, he will refuse to explain what kind of degree an "XyZ" is. He'll think you just need to get out more. (But don't we all?)

Coming soon to a theater near you (if there are any left)... *Adams Laws, the Sequel*, staring (in large letters) no one you've ever heard of, but we'll make the lettering *so* large, you'll be sure it's your failing, rather than that the actor is new.